LITTLE SECRETS* OF THE AUTO INDUSTRY

Hidden Warranties Cost Billions of Dollars

*The expression, secret warranty, is not one used by auto companies—they hate the term. Auto companies substitute "policy adjustments," "good will programs," or "extended warranties" for what is really a secret warranty. Whatever they are called, they are a longstanding industry practice. When a car company has a major defect that is not covered by the written factory warranty or that occurs after its factory warranty expires, it establishes an adjustment policy to pay for repairs rather than deal with thousands of complaints on a case by case basis. But the auto company communicates the policy to regional offices and sometimes to its dealers; it never notifies the customer so only those who complain loudly enough get covered by the secret warranty. The rest end up bearing the costs of the manufacturer's mistakes. (See page 2.)

LITTLE SECRETS OF THE AUTO INDUSTRY

Hidden Warranties Cost Billions of Dollars

CLARENCE DITLOW
and
RAY GOLD

MOYER BELL
Wakefield, Rhode Island & London

Published by Moyer Bell
Copyright © 1994 by Center for Auto Safety

First Edition

**LIBRARY OF CONGRESS
CATALOGING IN PUBLICATION DATA**

Ditlow, Clarence, Little secrets of the auto industry: hidden
warranties cost billions of dollars/by Clarence Ditlow and
Ray Gold.—1st ed.

p.   cm.
1. Automobile industry and trade—United States—corrupt
practices. 2. Warranty—United States. 3. Consumer
protection—United States. I. Gold, Ray. II. Title

HD9710.U52D53	1993
364.1'68—dc	93-22698
	CIP

ISBN 1-55921-102-4;
ISBN 1-55921-085-0 (pbk.)

Printed in the United States of America.
Distributed in North America by Publishers Group
West, P.O. Box 8843, Emeryville, CA 94662 800-
788-3123 (in California 510-658-3453) and by Ga-
zelle Book Services Ltd., Falcon House, Queen
Square, Lancaster LA1 1RN England.

Dedication

To the staff of the Cleveland regional office of the Federal Trade Commission including Paul Peterson, Paul Turley, Paul Eyre, Larry Green, Steve Benowitz, and Mel Wolowitz, we dedicate this book. This little office stood up for the average citizen against the giant auto companies and saved consumers billions of dollars in costly auto repairs. Their ceaseless work to expose secret warranties in the late 1970s and early 1980s set an example for how government should work.

CONTENTS

FOREWORD

This is a remarkable book, indeed; an all-in-one package of consumer justice. It combines the good story-telling of a first rate investigative exposé; the sound policy prescription of a pragmatic citizen advocacy agenda; and a bright-line clear consumer guide to millions of dollars in savings—and simple justice—for those American consumers who keep their cars for a while in the vain expectation that they won't fall apart the moment the warranty expires!

There are villains and heros aplenty in this story: auto companies who hold out the hope of fixing post-warranty defects—then set an impossible obstacle course for any, but the most intrepid consumer. A government agency—the FTC—which does its job faithfully and efficiently in bringing practical aid to consumers—hundreds of millions of dollars in relief—only to be handcuffed by the turn of the political wheel and the ascendancy of the Reagan Administration. In the 1980s "getting government off the backs of American Citizens" meant getting the government off the track of miscreant auto manufacturers—and jerking relief from the hands of citizens.

The FTC in the 1970s did its duty to auto consumers. And I'm proud of that. But I did little but get out of the way of a remarkable band of public servants: the staff of the FTC's Cleveland regional office. In this time of cynicism—even hatred—of government, of deep skepticism that government can or will do anything right or well, this book's heros include, yes, government bureaucrats and lawyers—not in Washington—but in the field, underfunded and underappreciated.

But, as good and dedicated as the FTC's Cleveland staff were, they would never have been educated or moved to investigate and act without the informed, expert advocacy of the Center For Auto Safety (CAS). It was with CAS that this investigation took root. It was CAS that pressed us at the FTC to act—and helped us find the way. It was CAS that kept up the pressure to make sure that remedial dollars reached the consumers' pockets. And it is CAS that today, abandoned by the FTC thus far into the 1990s, keeps up the good fight: in the state legislatures, in the courts, in Congress, in the Clinton Administration.

And with this book, CAS places in the hands of every concerned citizen/consumer the means to protect herself in the marketplace, and to pursue consumer justice for all consumers in the political marketplace.

—Michael Pertschuk

ACKNOWLEDGMENTS

It is difficult in a brief acknowledgment to express the full appreciation we owe to the many people who contributed their efforts to the production of this book.

For editing and offering tips on how to make the book more understandable to those without a legal background, we thank Irene Nagaraj of the Center for Auto Safety (CAS).

For editing and research into small claims courts across the country and several other matters, we thank Melissa Goldstein, a legal intern at CAS.

For editing, we thank Faith Little at CAS.

For his assistance in collecting manufacturer's materials and offering advice on secret warranties, we thank Robert Heimrehl of CAS.

For research and historical reference, we thank Debra Barclay.

For his assistance in writing a model state secret warranty law, we thank Mark Steinbach, a former CAS staff attorney and current lemon lawyer.

For her assistance in preparing the manufacturers' materials, we thank Elizabeth Cutler, a former member of the CAS staff.

For his legal research concerning limitation of the implied warranties and consumers' rights to consequential and incidental damages, we thank Michael Hardin, a former legal intern at CAS.

For their support and encouragement, we thank the rest of the staff at CAS.

Finally, we thank the thousands of frustrated and angry consumers who shared their problems with us. Their determination to fight for their rights will help future consumers seek the secret warranty relief they deserve.

LITTLE SECRETS OF THE AUTO INDUSTRY

Hidden Warranties Cost Billions of Dollars

CHAPTER 1

SECRET WARRANTIES AND YOU

Secret warranties are a multi-billion dollar consumer abuse. Every auto company issues secret warranties because every auto company makes mistakes in building cars. Sometimes these mistakes are design defects that affect every car of one model; sometimes the mistakes are manufacturing defects that affect only some cars. In either case, the defect must be repaired and the only question is who pays for the manufacturer's mistakes: the manufacturer or the consumer? Auto manufacturers often establish secret warranties to cover the cost of a repair, but the consumer has to be aware of the secret warranty in the first place, and be persistent in insisting that it be used to pay for his/her specific problem. This book will help you learn how to find out about these little secrets of the auto industry and how to get the manufacturer to apply them to your defect and pay for its mistake.

In 1987 the Center for Auto Safety (CAS) in Washington, D.C. made national headlines by identifying ten serious secret warranties covering 30 million vehicles estimated at costing $3 billion in repairs. This is just the tip of the iceberg. Over 500 secret warranties, from all auto companies, exist at any one time. One Toyota whistleblower alone provided a complete list in May 1988 of 41 secret warranties issued by that company.

Exposing secret warranties forces manufacturers to pay for

their mistakes. Having to foot the bill creates a strong incentive for them to build better cars in the future. And once secret warranties are disclosed, consumers save millions of dollars in repair bills. Since the CAS exposé, state legislatures have moved to pass secret warranty disclosure laws that will protect consumers. Until every state has passed these laws, consumers must rely on the strategies presented in this book to discover what secret warranties exist and how to make use of secret warranties to pay for repairs in their vehicles.

WHAT IS A SECRET WARRANTY?

The expression, secret warranty, is not one used by auto companies—they hate the term. Auto companies substitute "policy adjustments," "good will programs," or "extended warranties" for what is really a secret warranty. Whatever they are called, they are a longstanding industry practice. When a car company has a major defect that is not covered by the written factory warranty or that occurs after its factory warranty expires, it establishes an adjustment policy to pay for repairs rather than deal with thousands of complaints on a case by case basis. But the auto company communicates the policy to regional offices and sometimes to its dealers; it never notifies the customer so only those who complain loudly enough get covered by the secret warranty. The rest end up bearing the costs of the manufacturer's mistakes.

EXAMPLES OF SECRET WARRANTIES

CAS has documented case after case of secret warranties since its founding in 1970. One of the first and most famous was Ford's J-67 "Limited Service Program" which covered rust on 12 million 1969–72 cars and trucks. In this case a bulletin was sent only to Ford regional offices that stated, "This is a limited service program without dealership notification and should be administered on an individual complaint basis." Under this program, Ford would pay up to 100% to repair rust and paint damage on its vehicles even if the costs exceeded $1000. Showing that there is nothing new under the hood, in 1994 Ford has a secret warranty for peeling paint on millions of its 1985–92 models that could easily cost over $1 billion to repair.

All auto companies have been found to have secret warranties with little difference in the way they are applied and the reason for their existence. A 1972 Mazda secret warranty bulletin doubled the coverage for rotary engine damage but cautioned, "Since this is a temporary program which may be terminated at [any] time, owners are *not* to be informed of the extended coverage." Honda had secret warranties on head gaskets and rusting fenders in the mid-1970s; Chrysler had rusting fenders on Volares and Aspens in the late 1970s; GM had a transmission secret warranty caused by an international ban on sperm whale oil as a lubricant; Peugeot and Subaru both covered defective head gaskets; and VW's secret warranties covered valve stem seals.

Secret warranties soared after 1980 when the federal government dropped all efforts to eliminate them. GM had a 5 year/50,000 mile secret warranty covering repair of defective rack and pinion power steering systems on all 16 million of its 1981–88 front wheel drive cars.

Toyota covered pulsating brakes on its 1983–86 Camrys in a $100 million secret warranty.

Ford never told owners of its 1985–92 F-series pickups that America's most popular truck had peeling paint because Ford skipped the primer layer.

According to Nissan documents sent to CAS by a whistleblower in 1990, Nissan had at one time up to 48 secret warranties covering various cars and trucks.

There is no doubt that auto manufacturers presently have issued hundreds of secret warranties. It is difficult to know the exact number of secret warranties and to assess the magnitude of the practice because the warranties, by definition, are not intended for public disclosure. One Honda insider told CAS that Honda had at one time only one secret warranty book for each of its regions. The book was chained to a desk. Every page had the region's number superimposed on it so that any photocopy of a book page would show the region from which it came.

No Uniform Law Requires Secret Warranty Disclosure

There is no federal law that requires auto companies to disclose secret warranties. In the late 1970s, the Federal Trade Commission (FTC) sought to litigate individual secret warranties against each auto company beginning with a case of piston scuffing and cracked blocks in 1976–78 Fords. The FTC settled its case by requiring Ford to notify and directly compensate owners according to the secret warranty policy and to notify all future owners until the consent agreement expired eight years later in 1988. Although the FTC later filed similar complaints and actions against GM, VW, Honda, and Chrysler in the late 1970s, it dropped the requirement of secret warranty notification. In 1981 after the change of administrations, the commission completely dropped its efforts to expose secret warranties.

When a secret warranty exists, it is possible for consumers to band together to file a class action lawsuit against the manufacturer for an unfair trade practice. But this is a major effort which is rarely used and is a poor substitute for a disclosure law. In 1989, CAS helped the Center for Law in the Public Interest successfully sue Toyota over a secret warranty that covered up to $1800 in repair costs for pulsating brakes in over 400,000 1983–87 Camrys. To settle the class action, Toyota agreed to notify all present and past owners, to reimburse consumers for all repair expenses already incurred, and to repair all cars with the defect that had not yet been repaired. CAS estimated the total cost to Toyota to be over $100 million, most of which would have been borne by consumers had the class action not been brought.

STATE SECRET WARRANTY LAWS

In order to protect consumers from undisclosed defects, four states—California, Connecticut, Virginia, and Wisconsin—have enacted secret warranty laws, and many other states are now considering secret warranty legislation. The state secret warranty laws already enacted require manufacturers to disclose their "warranty adjustment" programs by giving direct notice of any warranty extension to affected owners, including information about the terms of the warranty, and provision for reimbursement to consumers who already have paid for the covered repair.

HOW TO FIND A SECRET WARRANTY

Until secret warranty disclosure laws become the law of the land, the only way to find out about secret warranties requires plain hard work. First you must check the technical service bulletins at your dealer's office for news on your vehicle type and model year. Service bulletins are published by the manufacturer and sent to dealerships to assist them in diagnosing and repairing problems on the vehicles they service. The existence of a service bulletin does not conclusively prove the auto company has a secret warranty, but it does signal a defect or problem for which the manufacturer has had to offer a repair.

Service bulletins can be difficult to decipher, but it is well worth the effort to try. Finding the right bulletin could save you thousands of dollars in repair costs. The right bulletin is the one that tells the dealer how to diagnose and fix a problem. It also will authorize the dealer to make repairs at the manufacturer's expense even when the defect is no longer or never was covered by the manufacturer's written factory warranty.

Often the permission to authorize free repair is only provided in the technical service bulletin sent to the factory representatives so that both the dealer and consumer are kept in the dark. Watch for code words in bulletins such as "check for availability of good will assistance." Companies often use such language to get around the triggering requirements for customer notification in states that have secret warranty disclosure laws.

Secret warranties often come to light when owners of vehicles of the same type and age are treated differently by the dealer or manufacturer. If some owners get their vehicles repaired at no cost or at a discount and other owners of the same vehicle do not, it is possible that a secret warranty exists to cover the defect involved. However, it is also possible that the dealer or manufacturer has decided to reimburse a relatively small number of owners on a case-by-case basis to retain their goodwill and not as part of a warranty adjustment program. To constitute a secret warranty, the difference in treatment of customers must be based on a corporate policy to reimburse owners that is communicated to regional offices and usually also to dealers but that is not communicated to consumers.

HOW TO USE A SECRET WARRANTY

Once you have determined that your vehicle is covered by a secret warranty, the next step is to take the service bulletin that proves the existence of the secret warranty with you when you go to your dealer to get the defect repaired. Without the bulletin, you will have a much more difficult time convincing the dealer that he should repair your vehicle free of charge. Even if the dealer refuses to recognize the existence of the secret warranty (he might not know that the secret warranty exists) or if your vehicle is beyond the period of coverage of the secret warranty, he still may repair your vehicle at no expense as part of a goodwill adjustment.

If the dealer claims your vehicle is not covered by a secret warranty and refuses to give you a goodwill adjustment, your next step is to pursue your claim directly with the manufacturer. You should do this for two reasons. First, unlike dealers, the manufacturer will always know if a certain defect in one of its own vehicles is covered by a secret warranty. Second, every manufacturer has a system to handle consumer complaints which should be followed even though it may not work in most cases. Complaint handling mechanisms outside the manufacturer's system (e.g. arbitration) require exhaustion of all remedies that the manufacturer provides. Do not move onto legal action until you have followed the manufacturer's complaint handling system to no avail.

Contact the manufacturer's division (also called regional, district or zone) office in your area. The locations and correct names of district offices and the complaint procedures are often provided in your car's owner's manual. If the manufacturer's representative refuses to see you, contact the regional office or the manufacturer's owner relations office, often located in Detroit.

If the manufacturer refuses to extend the secret warranty to your vehicle (perhaps because your car is beyond the time or mileage requirements of the secret warranty), do not give up. Manufacturers only reimburse those owners who complain loudly and persistently; those who put off complaining, or who never complain at all, must pay for the manufacturer's mistakes.

The next step is to make enough noise outside the manufacturer's complaint handling system to get results. A strong commitment is necessary to use this procedure successfully because you will not get results unless you are willing to be persistent with follow-up letters and phone calls. Complain in writing to the manufacturer's chairman of the board or president with copies of your letter to others. Describe the defect covered by the secret warranty clearly and precisely within the letter and refer to the collected documentation of the car's troubles and your attempts to have the car repaired "within the system."

Send copies to various organizations such as local and national consumer groups, local and state consumer protection agencies, state attorneys general, federal agencies and members of Congress. Even if these agencies or groups cannot act directly on your behalf, they may send complaints on to the manufacturer requesting that the manufacturer take action.

Tell the local media about your secret warranty problem. Many consumers get reimbursed because a local Action Line, newspaper or television station starts to take an interest in a secret warranty. After all, if a manufacturer is trying to keep a secret warranty secret, the last thing the company wants is publicity on the secret warranty. A particularly good strategy is to announce the formation of a group to expose the particular secret warranty affecting your car. Even if the group is as small as you and your neighbor, a group is more powerful and attracts more attention than an individual.

SMALL CLAIMS COURT

Manufacturers often stonewall the consumer over secret warranties knowing that many consumers will give up in utter frustration and go away. Don't. Take the documentation on the secret warranty and your repair efforts to small claims court. At this point, it's the manufacturer who often gives in knowing that the legal rights are on the consumer's side. The manufacturer relies on its own lengthy complaint handling mechanism to wear down consumers. Once you show you won't be beat by this mechanism, you should succeed in your efforts to get the manufacturer to pay.

The old adage "the squeaky wheel gets the grease" holds true for getting a secret warranty applied to your defective car. The consumers who complain the loudest get reimbursed. The quiet customer who goes away quietly gets ripped off. Until auto companies genuinely believe that consumer protection is good business, consumers have to be aggressive to protect their rights or they will wind up paying for an auto company's mistake. Since billions of dollars in repairs are covered by secret warranties, the total benefit to consumers of discovering them is enormous.

CHAPTER 2

WHAT IS A SECRET WARRANTY?

February 19, 1993

Pontiac Motor Division-General Motors Corporation
Attention: Customer Service Manager
Pontiac, Michigan 48340

Dear Pontiac:

In August 1986, my husband and I purchased a brand new midnight blue Pontiac Firebird. We were both very excited and loved our new sports car. We were both a little upset that within one year, the inside console by the gear shift came loose and was not sealed correctly. Of course we were never prepared for what would happen next to our shiny new sports car.

We both noticed on the back spoiler a small spot in the paint that was fading. We thought this should not happen with a vehicle which is not even two years old. But we thought it was minor and we could just get the spot touched up with paint. But the spot spread until the whole spoiler and rear bumper was a white chalky blue color. We contacted the dealer who sold us the car. The dealer told us this was not unusual and sometimes a fading can occur.

Since our car was no longer under warranty there was nothing they could do.

Well the problem did not stop there. Within the same year spots started on the hood and top of the car. Soon the entire hood and top looked just as bad as the back of the car. I contacted several other Pontiac dealers and was told basically the same thing. Natural causes must have caused the fading and there was nothing they could do about it. Well we were quite disappointed since my husband and I had three children and we were living on one income and could not afford a new paint job for our Firebird.

A friend read an article in the *Indianapolis Star* in January 1993 of the problems with the paint in General Motors cars dating back to 1986. We were quite relieved to find out we were right all along that there was a defect with the paint. We had had several cars over ten years old before owning the Firebird and had never had any problem with fading paint. To purchase a brand new vehicle to only have it look like an ugly vehicle within three years is very upsetting.

We finally thought our problem would be solved. We took the Firebird into a local dealer and was told by the General Service Manager within a quick glance of our car, that yes it was caused by defective paint. To our surprise, he said since the car was more than six years old there was nothing they could do. Since we were not notified of a possible defect by any Pontiac dealer or representative we have to pay the full $1500 to get our Firebird repainted. Not satisfied with this situation, I talked with Patty at Pontiac customer assistance. After waiting two weeks she told me the same thing; there is nothing Pontiac will do to correct their defect.

I still cannot believe a corporation as large as General

Motors knowing of defects in their cars, would not do anything to remedy the problem for the customer. We are totally disappointed, outraged, and frustrated with the run-around we seem to have received by Pontiac. We know this is *not* right and we do plan to pursue this matter.

Sincerely,
L. and D. Dew
San Antonio, Texas

What happened to Laura and David Dew happens to many consumers across the U.S. every year. Their vehicle suffered from a defect for years. They complained to the manufacturer without success. Then they discovered there was a secret warranty on their vehicle that should have covered the repair. But by the time they found out about the secret warranty, their vehicle was no longer covered and the manufacturer turned them down saying in essence, "Sorry, you're too late." The manufacturer's secret warranty did exactly what it is supposed to do—make you pay for its engineering mistakes.

Other consumers with almost identical problems get far different results. Some consumers with 1986 GM vehicles with peeling paint got GM to take care of repairs even though their vehicles were over six years old by 1993.

January 27, 1993

Dear Center:

My original letter to GM was responded to by the GM Customer Assistance Department with a cursory "brush-off" indicating that the problem was the result of age or mileage and that Chevrolet would offer no assistance.

After receiving the letters from the Center for Auto Safety and doing further investigative work of my own, I sent a second, considerably more vituperative demand letter to GM. Again, GM dismissed my complaints.

I compiled a list of other people with similar problems and was getting ready to go to the attorney general when I got a call from GM who had suddenly adopted an unexpectedly conciliatory attitude. To make a long story short, GM had my 1986 van inspected at a local dealer and agreed to pay the $2,000 total cost of repainting it.

Sincerely,
R. Brazell
Corpus Christi, Texas

THE DEFINITION OF A SECRET WARRANTY

The term "secret warranty" is used to describe the practice by which automobile manufacturers establish a policy to pay for repair of defects not covered by the original factory warranty (express warranty). Most often, this involves paying for repairs after the express warranty has expired but sometimes it involves paying for repairs, such as brake pads, that are not covered by the factory warranty. In all cases, owners or customers are *not* notified. The conditions covered by secret warranties often result from defects in material or workmanship that appear only after expiration of the written warranty.

Secret warranties share three elements: first, the existence of a common defect recognized by a manufacturer; second, the establishment of a policy to pay for all or part of the cost of repair of the defect beyond the terms of the express factory warranty; and third, the failure of the manufacturer to notify directly vehicle owners about the "warranty" or policy adjustment. Since the manufacturer doesn't notify the consumer, only the consumer who complains loudly enough gets covered by the secret warranty. Other consumers end up bearing the costs of the manufacturer's mistakes because they pay for the repairs themselves.

DUCK TEST FOR SECRET WARRANTIES

Auto companies hate the term "secret warranty." They prefer to use the phrase "policy adjustment" or "good will program" or "extended warranty." In response to auto company evasiveness on the existence of secret warranties, the Center for Auto Safety applies the "Duck Test": If it looks like a duck, quacks like a duck, and waddles like a duck, then it is a duck. If a manufacturer has a vehicle with a widespread defect, pays all or part of the repair cost beyond repairs provided for in the express warranty, and fails to notify owners, then it's a secret warranty.

WHY AND HOW SECRET
WARRANTIES ARE CREATED

Secret warranties typically are created when a manufacturer realizes that a large number of customers are experiencing the same condition or defect. It then issues instructions to its regional offices and/or dealers on how to deal with the particular problem. By notifying only the regional office and/or dealers, it eliminates the need to respond to what otherwise might be tens or hundreds of thousands of individual requests for "goodwill adjustments."

Auto makers do agree to pay for some post-warranty repairs to stand behind their products and minimize consumer dissatisfaction. But notifying all affected vehicle owners that a defective component would be repaired without charge could entail considerable expense. So rather than "extending" the warranty to all owners whose vehicles manifest a widespread defect, manufacturers notify only their regional offices and/or dealers about the warranty so they only have to reimburse those consumers who complain loudly enough; the nice quiet consumer pays for the manufacturer's mistake.

Typically under such programs, repairs will be made or reimbursed only when the vehicle owner reports the problem within a designated time period, such as the first five years or 50,000 miles. Some secret warranties, however, have extended for the life of the car.

GOOD WILL ADJUSTMENT
VERSUS SECRET WARRANTIES

Consumers frequently complain to manufacturers about defects and failures not covered by the express written warranty, especially ones surfacing soon after expiration of the written warranty. Auto makers must respond quickly to each request or they risk losing customers.

Auto makers have two distinctly different types of customer assistance programs to respond to such problems: *good will adjustments* to take care of the *isolated* failure due to a random flaw that happens after the warranty expires; and *secret warranties* that cover *systematic defects* that occur in many vehicles due to an engineering mistake. Auto companies often try to disguise secret warranties as good will adjustments to avoid their disclosure.

For the random failure, the auto company makes a case-by-case decision about repairing the vehicle in order to maintain the customer's good will. The auto maker takes many factors into account before deciding to repair a vehicle: how the customer has maintained his or her car, how clean the car is, and other indications of the care the customer has taken of the vehicle. They examine the car to see if the owner has abused it or used the car for purposes not intended. They also may check on how many of the manufacturer's cars a customer and family members have purchased over the years.

When a model has a component that has a high failure rate, the volume of requests for repair is enormous. Auto makers will then notify regional offices and dealers and instruct them on handling the response to consumers' requests for repairs. If manufacturers had to make a decision to authorize free repairs on common defects on a case-by-case basis, they would quickly be overwhelmed by the number of complaints. Hence the majority of these problems are kept secret and become secret warranties.

Auto makers that acknowledge the use of secret warranties allege that they are a constructive and socially useful component of their customer relations programs but they must remain secret to be effective: at least *some* customers get free repairs who would otherwise have had to pay for them. Auto companies contend that if they had to disclose secret warranties and pay for all the repairs, they would eliminate the secret warranties altogether.

WHAT'S WRONG WITH "SECRET WARRANTIES"?

Secret warranties are deceptive and unfair. They force consumers to pay for manufacturers' mistakes and the repairs are often more costly because the problem was not revealed, and repaired, in a timely fashion.

Consumers pay billions of dollars each year for repairs covered by secret warranties. If auto companies were forced to absorb this cost, they would move quickly to build higher quality vehicles to avoid paying the repair cost for their mistakes. As long as the consumer pays for the cost of defects covered by secret warranties, manufacturers have no economic incentive to eliminate the defects. Auto companies additionally profit from defects covered by secret warranties through the sale of repair parts to fix the defects.

What is a Secret Warranty?

When a manufacturer knows of a common, material defect in new cars, it is a deceptive trade practice to keep that knowledge secret from its customers.

When Ford discovered that paint was peeling from its F-series pickups in 1987 because it had omitted a primer layer, Ford could not correct the problem at all of its manufacturing plants until 1993. Yet Ford continued through 1993 to sell new pickups that could have their paint peel—without telling new pickup buyers.

It is not only unfair and wasteful, but costly when a manufacturer knows of defects which, if not repaired, will cause expensive problems in the future. When the manufacturer fails to advise consumers of the defect they have no opportunity to prevent the likely future repair.

TIMING BELT FIASCO—OOPS, THERE GOES ANOTHER ENGINE

A prime example of this problem is timing belt or chain failure. Car companies used to use rugged metal timing chains that seldom failed. Now many companies used plastic timing belts that can fail prematurely. Failure is particularly common in the smaller, higher performance engines that run at higher RPM's. Replacing a timing belt may cost $200. But if it fails in use, it may cause extensive engine damage costing several thousands of dollars to repair.

Norm and Debbie Harkins of Las Vegas may hold the record for engine damage when the timing chain broke at 67,000 miles on their 1982 Mercedes 380SL. As Mrs. Harkins wrote CAS:

> I backed the 380SL out of our driveway, proceeded to the end of the block when I heard a little ping and the

engine just quit. We called the Mercedes dealer to tow our car into the shop. According to the dealer, the 380SL has a single timing chain which broke and scored the block.

We told them to go ahead and fix it. That's when the *shock* came. It cost $14,763 to repair. Mercedes paid $6,398 and we had to pay $8,365. We could not believe Mercedes would not back up their product 100%. We never missed an oil change, tune-up, etc. Whatever the car required for maintenance, we took care of and have all the service slips to prove it.

Although many new car owner manuals today tell owners to replace timing belts at 60,000 miles as part of the required maintenance, few did so in the 1980s. As a result many owners of cars experience costly engine failures when their timing belts break. Auto companies handled this problem in widely divergent ways. Ford, for instance, notified owners of the timing belt failure and paid for repairs. Chrysler established a secret warranty, and Honda notified owners that the belts needed replacing but told owners they had to pay for them.

In every case, the car companies should have paid for timing belt replacement and any engine repairs that resulted from the failure. Consumers report having to replace engines at a cost of $2,000-3,000 apiece.

CAS reported in 1984 that it had received numerous complaints of timing belt failure from owners of 1981–83 Ford Escorts and Mercury Lynxes. When failure occurred beyond two years and 24,000 miles (the time covered by the written warranty), Ford had paid *only* those owners who had complained most loudly. Under pressure from CAS, Ford wrote all owners of 1981–83 Ford Escorts and Mercury Lynxes that Ford would pay for new timing belts and engine repairs through the first five years and 60,000 miles. (See copy of Ford's letter, page 20.)

What is a Secret Warranty?

J. P. King
Manager
Service Engineering Office
Ford Parts and Service Division

Ford Motor Company
3000 Schaefer Road
P.O. Box 1904
Dearborn, Michigan 48121

April, 1984

Dear Owner:

This is to advise you of a special service program covering engine timing belt repairs on 1981, 1982 and certain 1983-model Escort, Lynx, EXP and LN7 vehicles. We also want to remind you of the importance of the scheduled maintenance that is required for the timing belt at 60,000 miles. Our records indicate that you own a vehicle covered by the program. The vehicle serial number is shown on the envelope that contained this letter. (If you own more than one affected vehicle, the serial numbers are shown on a listing enclosed with this letter.)

Description Of The Condition:

In a small number of these vehicles the engine timing belts have broken prior to 60,000 miles. At that point, belt replacement is required as part of your vehicle's scheduled maintenance. Timing belt breakage appears to be more prevalent in warmer climates and where an engine is run at idle for long periods. In some instances, particularly at high engine speeds, breakage of the timing belt has resulted in costly engine repairs. Timing belts currently in use in production have been improved and these changes are also incorporated in genuine Ford service replacement belts.

Ford's Program:

If the timing belt on your vehicle breaks prior to five years from your vehicle's in-service date or 60,000 miles of operation, whichever comes first, Ford will replace the timing belt at no charge to you. Engine repairs resulting from timing belt breakage also are covered by the program. Timing belt replacement for other reasons is not covered by this program.

Actions You Should Take:

If your vehicle is approaching 60,000 miles or has passed that mileage, you should plan to have the timing belt replaced promptly as part of its scheduled maintenance. This could help prevent the inconvenience and expense you could incur if the timing belt were to break, resulting in a damaged and inoperative engine. The cost of replacing the timing belt for maintenance or for other than belt failure is the responsibility of the owner.

To Have This Service Performed:

Should the engine timing belt on your vehicle break, contact any Ford or Lincoln-Mercury dealership to arrange an appointment for service. All dealerships in your area have been advised of this program, and can assist you as necessary.

Reimbursement For Prior Repairs:

If you have already had a broken timing belt replaced on your vehicle at your expense within 60,000 miles of service, Ford will reimburse you. This reimbursement will cover the cost of replacing the belt and of other repairs resulting from belt breakage. Reimbursement includes the deductible amount you may have paid under Ford Motor Company's 24 month/24,000 mile powertrain warranty, Ford's Extended Service Plan (ESP), or any similar plan in effect on your vehicle.

To request reimbursement, present your paid repair order or over-the-counter parts purchase receipt to any Ford or Lincoln-Mercury dealership by October 31, 1984. The dealership will make arrangements to reimburse you for the costs you incurred.

Ford Motor Company is taking this action as part of our ongoing effort to maintain owner confidence in our products. We want you to be satisfied with your Ford-built vehicle, and we look forward to keeping you as a customer.

Sincerely,

J. P. King
Service Engineering Office Manager

M31

What is a Secret Warranty?

Toyota notified 1983–84 Camry owners that their timing belts were subject to failure and to bring them in for inspection and replacement as necessary. Unlike Ford, Toyota did not offer to pay for engine damage for any vehicles with mileage greater than provided for by the express written warranty. However, if owners complained loudly, engine damage was repaired under a secret warranty. (See page 23 for Toyota letter.)

In 1987, Honda wrote owners of 1984–85 models about a maintenance schedule revision requiring installation of an "improved" timing belt at 60,000 miles but said owners would have to pay the $150 cost. The defect first showed up in the 1983 Prelude when Honda made an engine design change. Honda notified 1983 Prelude owners and offered to replace the belt free of charge but apparently changed its mind for later model years when the cost of replacing the belt became much higher.

Gary Magness of Dallas was driving down the road in his 1984 Prelude when the timing belt failed without warning. All eight intake valves had to be replaced resulting in $800 in engine damage. The car had been driven 54,000 miles. At first, Mr. Magness paid the repair bill. After he complained loudly about the failure to Honda's regional office in Irving, Texas, Honda agreed to reimburse him for the $800 repair bill. (See page 24 for Honda letter.)

Chrysler adopted a policy of total consumer secrecy when it found the timing chain guide was failing on the 2.6 liter 4-cylinder engine made by Mitsubishi, one of the main engines used in Chrysler's 1981–84 cars and vans. The chain guide failed because of a blocked oil feed. Chrysler redesigned the lubrication system and notified dealers of the problem and new repair procedure but failed to notify owners who often had the timing chain and the chain guide fail with resultant engine damage. Once again, only owners who complained loudly enough got reimbursed under a secret warranty policy.

TOYOTA

TOYOTA MOTOR SALES, U.S.A., INC.

NOVEMBER, 1984

Dear Toyota Camry Owner:

In support of our commitment to consumer satisfaction, Toyota will commence to inspect all 1983 and some 1984 Toyota Camry vehicles. This service campaign is to check your Camry engine timing belt and replace the belt if necessary.

Toyota has determined that some of the timing belts, which drives the valve camshaft from the crankshaft, may be subject to excessive wear and failure under extended mileage conditions.

To prevent the possibility of this condition occurring on your vehicle please contact your Toyota Dealer immediately and make arrangements to have your Camry inspected. The inspection and/or replacement will be at no cost to you. If the timing belt replacement is required it will take approximately 2.5 hours of actual labor time to complete the repair.

All Toyota dealers are provided with detailed instructions for this service campaign and are ready to perform this service.

Our files indicate that you may own one of the subject Camry vehicles. However if you have sold or traded your vehicle, please let us know by completing the postage paid owner information card enclosed.

Toyota is taking this action as part of our ongoing efforts to maintain owner confidence and satisfaction in our products. We sincerely regret any inconvenience this may cause you.

TOYOTA MOTOR SALES, U.S.A., INC.
CORPORATE SERVICE DEPARTMENT

What is a Secret Warranty?

COPY

October 16, 1987

Dear Honda Owner,

To enhance vehicle durability at extended mileage, we have added CAMSHAFT TIMING BELT REPLACEMENT to the 1984 and 1985 Accord, Civic and Prelude Maintenance Schedules. The timing belt should be replaced at or before the 60,000 mile scheduled maintenance. If the mileage on your vehicle is near or beyond 60,000 miles, you should make an appointment to have the timing belt replaced.

The cost of this belt replacement, like any other maintenance item, will be your responsibility; it is not a warranty item.

Since the camshaft timing belt is a primary engine component, this maintenance is important to help ensure the long-term reliability of your engine.

Once an improved Genuine Honda timing belt has been installed, it will normally not need to be replaced again because of improvements in belt technology. If your dealer has already replaced your timing belt as part of a scheduled service, please disregard this letter. As a courtesy to future owners, please indicate that your Honda has the new timing belt installed by noting the change in the Owner's Manual Maintenance Section. Your dealer will also inspect the condition of the water pump, which is readily accessible when replacing the timing belt. If the condition of the pump is questionable, we urge that you have it replaced at the same time.

The labor times and parts costs shown in the table below are estimates and may vary. Contact your dealer for an actual cost estimate.

Item	Suggested Honda Labor Time (hours)			Suggested Honda Parts Cost
	Accord	Prelude	Civic	All
Camshaft Timing Belt Replacement	2.3	2.3	1.3	$30
Water Pump Replacement (If done when the timing belt is replaced)	Add 0.2	Add 0.2	Add 0.2	$35

If you plan on selling your car before it reaches 60,000 miles, as a courtesy to the next owner, please insert this letter in the Maintenance Schedule section of your Honda's Owner's Manual.

Thank you for your cooperation. This service is intended to help ensure your continued satisfaction with your Honda.

Sincerely,

AMERICAN HONDA MOTOR CO., INC.

ATB 1952 (8709)

John Chavanne of Redondo Beach, California ran into a stone wall at Chrysler when his daughter's timing chain failed. Then he got a little help from CAS. Mr. Chavanne reported:

> Thank you for the information on hidden warranties. I was able to help my daughter collect almost $700 from Chrysler on repairs to a defective timing chain in a 1984 Plymouth Voyager. They were not going to cover this repair until I quoted to them from their own service bulletin, which I obtained from CAS.

(See pages 26 and 27 for Chrysler technical service bulletin.)

Secret warranties are fundamentally unfair because manufacturers grant free repairs to some customers but not to others with identical problems. Only customers who complain persistently get the benefits of a secret warranty program. This runs contrary to the notion that persons similarly situated are entitled to similar treatment. The result is that billions of dollars worth of repairs are improperly shifted from manufacturers to individual customers.

Because many consumers take their cars to independent repair shops instead of the dealer after expiration of the written warranty, especially for expensive repair work, they have no opportunity to learn about or benefit from secret warranty programs. This harms both the consumer, who must pay for the repair, and potentially the manufacturer, whose customers are unhappy about the repair costs. Moreover, because the defects are often difficult to diagnose without repair instructions provided by manufacturers to their dealers, consumers will sometimes pay for unnecessary repairs due to mistaken diagnoses or failure of the independent shops to use the updated repair procedure.

Technical Service Bulletin

Technical Information +
Professional Service =
Customer Satisfaction

Of Interest ☐ General Manager ☐ Sales Manager ☐ Service Manager ☐ Parts Manager ☐ Service Technicians

Models

1981-1984 Ram Van
Caravan, Voyager;
Aries, Reliant;
LeBaron, Dodge 400
Dodge 600, E Class,
New Yorker 4-Dr.;
Dodge 600 2-Dr.,
Convertible w/2.6L
Engine

SYMPTOM/CONDITION

Rattle from the camshaft and silent shaft chain area at the front of the engine accompanied by a broken camshaft timing chain guide PN MD021231 (Figure 1).

DIAGNOSIS

Inspect for:

1. Blocked oil feed hole to the timing chain hydraulic chain tensioner located in the oil pump housing (Figure 2). Blockage occurs when a section of the oil pump mounting gasket collapses into the channel in the pump cover which directs oil from the main oil gallery in the block to the chain tensioner feed hole.

2. Lockwasher, PN MF450404, may also be missing from between silent shaft chain guide "B" pivot bolt and timing chain guide (Figure 3).

PARTS REQUIRED

1 - Oil Pump Mounting Gasket PN MD060521
1 - Lockwasher   PN MF450404
1 - Timing Chain Guide   PN MD021231

REPAIR PROCEDURE

1. Remove chain case cover, silent shaft chain, camshaft chain, and broken chain guide.

2. Remove engine oil pump and clean all traces of old mounting gasket from pump and engine block.

Subject

Camshaft Timing
Chain Guide
Breakage

Index

ENGINE

Date

January 7, 1985

No.

09-02-85

(THIS BULLETIN IS SUPPLIED AS
TECHNICAL INFORMATION ONLY
AND IS NOT AN AUTHORIZATION
FOR REPAIRS) REPRINT OF THIS
MATERIAL NOT AUTHORIZED
UNLESS APPROVED.

09-02-85   -2-

3. Obtain new gasket PN MD060521 and, using a sharp knife, rework by cutting out portion of gasket within dotted lines indicated in Figure 4.

    NOTE: DISREGARD REWORK INSTRUCTIONS IN STEP 3 IF NEW GASKET ALREADY HAS HOLE CUT OUT.

            THIS CHANGE WAS INCORPORATED IN ENGINES IN PRODUCTION, APPROXIMATELY 84-04-01, (ENGINE BUILD DATE, CODE 7-282), AND WILL BE IN SERVICE REPLACEMENT GASKETS AT A LATER DATE.

4. Reinstall pump using reworked mounting gasket.

5. Install new Timing Chain Guide PN MD021231.

6. Install timing chain, silent shaft chain, and guides according to instructions contained in the applicable service manual.

    NOTE: ENSURE THAT LOCKWASHER PN MF450404 IS IN PLACE AS INDICATED IN FIGURE 3.

7. Install chain case cover.

POLICY: Reimbursable within the provisions of the warranty

TIME ALLOWANCE:

Labor Operation No.			
	09-02-85-90	Camshaft Timing Chain Guide Breakage	3.9
	09-02-85-91	Optional Equipment Power Steering	0.1
	09-02-85-92	Optional Equipment Air Conditioning	0.2

FAILURE CODE: 68 - Noisy

R. Stone
Manager, Service Engineering

Illustrations

What is a Secret Warranty?

TYPES OF SECRET WARRANTIES

Warranty Time/Mileage Extension: Toyota Pulsating Brakes

One of the most common secret warranties is the simple extension of the time and mileage limits for items covered by the express warranty. For example, Toyota's basic warranty for brakes on mid-1980s models covered the cars for 12 months or 12,000 miles, whichever came first. In July 1987, Toyota extended the warranty to 36 months and 36,000 miles on 1983–87 Camrys for a defect that caused the brakes to pulsate when applied. The consumer experienced the problem as a pulsation or shudder in the steering. The defect led to excess tire wear and such severe deterioration of the front suspension that the lower control arms often had to be replaced along with the brake drums.

Toyota sent both a warranty bulletin and a service bulletin to its dealers about the brake pulsation problem in 1983-86 Camrys but never notified owners. (See the warranty bulletin on page 29.) Repairs covered by the bulletin ran as high as $1,000 per car. Although the Toyota warranty bulletin told dealers to "contact your district service manager for consideration of goodwill assistance for repairs beyond warranty guidelines," approval was automatic as long as the Camry was produced within the three and one-half year period specified in the bulletin.

Owners were never notified, however, prompting the Center for Law in the Public Interest to file a class action suit against Toyota. The company settled in 1988, agreeing to: (1) notify all past and present owners and lessees of the 400,000 cars covered by the suit of the defect; (2) reimburse consumers who already paid for brake pulsation repairs, including related incidental expenses such as rental cars and taxicabs; (3) repair any cars yet to be fixed and those that developed the defect within one year after the settlement; (4) pay a total of $835,000 to a Consumer Support and

TOYOTA

Warranty Bulletin

Date: 07-08-87   No: 87-28   Ref: _____

SUBJECT: Warranty Procedures for Camry Brake Pulsation Field Fix

The following guidelines should be used when submitting warranty claims for repairs to Camry brakes following the instructions distributed to dealers in TSB Volume VIII, #3 - revised.

Warranty coverage for the brake components on vehicles referenced in this TSB (1983 through 1986 model year) is 12 months/12,500 miles, whichever occurs first. Contact your district service manager for consideration of goodwill assistance for repairs to vehicles beyond these warranty guidelines.

Warranty claims for vehicles repaired according to the field fix procedures should be submitted as follows:

Opcode	Description	Labor
771011	Front brake and steering mainshaft replacement	6.8 hours
771012	Front brake, steering mainshaft and caliper replacement	7.3 hours
771013	Front brake, steering mainshaft, brake drum replacement and test drive	8.0 hours
771014	Front brake, steering mainshaft and caliper, brake drum replacement and test drive	8.6 hours

Original Part Number: Use the rotor as the original part number
Condition/Cause/Remedy: Describe repair in detail and reference TSB
#3-revised

If additional work is required (replacement of lower control arms, replacement of tires*), submit the additional time required on the same warranty claim using a "Z" combination code in the usual manner for claiming "Z" time. If portions of the repair must be sublet out by the dealer, claim those portions of the repair in the sublet section of the warranty claim.

If you have any questions regarding submission of these claims, please contact your district service manager.

* When performing tire replacements, please reference the Toyota Tire Warranty Reference Manual for detailed procedures.

WAM7275.8

SERVICE BULLETIN
TOYOTA MOTOR SALES, U.S.A., INC.

VOLUME

REFERENCE BRAKES
NUMBER 003 REVISED
DATE 08-07-87
MODEL SV1, CV1

TITLE CAMRY FRONT BRAKE PULSATION REPAIR PROCEDURE (Revised)

If it becomes necessary to repair a vehicle for brake pulsation, use the appropriate procedure listed in the Table below.

PRODUCTION DATE:

From	To	Procedure
January 1983	July 1985	A
August 1985	November 1985[1]	B
November 1985	August 1986[2]	A

(1)   **Starting VIN**   **Ending VIN**

  JT2SV1#**G0368501   JT2SV1#**G0410172
  JT2CV13E*G0000075   JT2CV13E*G0003254

(2)   **Starting VIN**   **Ending VIN**

  JT2SV1#**G0410173   JT2SV1#**G0524458
  JT2CV13E*G0003255   JT2CV13E*G0011149

TECHNICAL ASSURANCE DEPARTMENT

Education Fund; and (5) pay $250,000 in attorneys' fees. Total cost of the settlement: $100 million.

Inadequate Notification: GM Power Steering

Some manufacturers will put out a press release about a secret warranty and claim that this is adequate notification. They will often omit essential details, such as the model years covered under the secret warranty. Usually the release is put out in a fashion guaranteed to get as little coverage as possible: The manufacturer releases it on a Friday afternoon. As a result, many newspapers don't cover the story. If they do, it's often small and runs on a Saturday, so that most owners don't see it.

General Motors is a master at this technique and uses it frequently. Here is a typical example of how it works: GM experienced defective rack and pinion power steering systems on 16 million of its 1981–88 front wheel drive cars. The express warranty for steering covered up to 12 or 24 months and 12,000 to 24,000 miles depending on the model. But GM created a 5 year/50,000 mile secret warranty covering steering repair of these front wheel drive cars but only notified 1981 owners of the extension. These models are prone to loss of power assist for the rack and pinion steering assembly. In those vehicles with the defect, consumers frequently or occasionally lose the power steering and thus have difficulty turning their steering wheels. Usually, this loss of assist first occurs only when the engine is cold, but in time it becomes more noticeable after the car has warmed up. The defect occurred because GM used an aluminum valve body housing and teflon rings around the internal spool valve. The rings dug into the soft valve housing and permitted power steering fluid to leak past them when cold.

GM's own engineers recognized the mistake they made and recommended changes in 1982. But GM management refused to implement the changes which would have eliminated the problem by the 1984 model year. Instead GM waited until 1989 to fix the problem on the assembly line. In the intervening years, about 16 million cars were made with defective rack and pinion power steering systems. In the 1980s, no one stood behind its mistakes like GM—it just kept on making the same mistake year after year after year.

Under pressure from CAS, GM acknowledged the secret warranty on its 1982–1985 front-wheel-drive cars in a January 21, 1988 news release (see page 33). Then, in a May 25, 1989 news release (see page 34), it extended its secret warranty to include 1985–1988 front-wheel-drive cars. The second release was a masterpiece of evasion in that it did not even name the models affected.

GM never notified individual owners of the extended warranty and few consumers ever heard of the news releases or the free repairs on their cars. By the time many consumers learned of the secret warranty, the 5 year/50,000 limit had already expired. Even though many of these consumers had first experienced symptoms of the defect before the limit, they didn't take it in for repair because it was a relatively minor problem. Consumers waited until the car got very difficult to steer before getting it fixed. By then many consumers were beyond the limit and had to fight hard to get reimbursement.

The following are just a few examples of consumers who were fortunate enough to find out about this secret warranty from CAS.

> Thank you for saving a college student over $500 in repairs on my 1984 Pontiac Sunbird. The power steering defect caused my entire rack assembly to be completely destroyed. If your organization did not exist, I would never have known about this secret warranty.
>
> S. Brodsky
> Lowell, Massachusetts

GENERAL MOTORS CORPORATION
1660 L STREET, N. W.
WASHINGTON, D. C. 20036
(202) 775-5018

NEWS

IMMEDIATELY, THURSDAY, JANUARY 21, 1988

DETROIT -- General Motors is making available a special policy of five years or 50,000 miles to cover repair of a possible temporary reduction in power steering assist on certain front-wheel-drive cars produced between 1982 and 1985.

Some of the vehicles may experience reduced power steering assist upon first starting the car, primarily in cold weather. Once the system warms up -- usually in one or two minutes -- normal power steering assist is restored. The condition does not occur while the vehicle is being driven after warmup.

Under the special policy, GM will reimburse owners who in the past paid to have the condition corrected during the first five years or 50,000 miles of operation, provided they present proper receipts to their dealer. GM dealers also will repair free of charge power steering systems that exhibit the condition within the time and mileage limits of the special policy.

Included in the special policy are 1982-84 subcompact, compact and intermediate cars, and 1985 model full-size luxury cars.

Specific models included are as follows:

o 1982-84 Buick Skyhawk, Skylark and Century; Cadillac Cimarron; Chevrolet Cavalier, Citation and Celebrity; Oldsmobile Firenza, Omega and Cutlass Ciera and Pontiac Sunbird, Phoenix and 6000 models.

o 1985 Buick Electra, Cadillac DeVille and Oldsmobile Ninety-Eight models.

########

What is a Secret Warranty?

GENERAL MOTORS CORPORATION
1660 L STREET, N. W.
WASHINGTON, D. C. 20036
(202) 775-5012

NEWS

IMMEDIATELY, THURSDAY, May 25, 1989

DETROIT — In the interest of continued customer satisfaction, General Motors is extending its five-year/50,000-mile special policy — covering free repair of a possible temporary initial reduction in power steering assist — to include certain front-wheel drive cars produced between 1985 and 1988.

The limited warranty on power steering systems for these GM cars was for one year or 12,000 miles.

Some of the vehicles may experience reduced power steering assist upon first starting the car, primarily in cold weather. Once the system warms up — usually in one or two minutes — normal power steering assist is restored. The condition does not occur while the vehicle is being driven after warmup.

Under the special policy, GM dealers will repair free of charge power steering systems that exhibit the problem during the first five years or 50,000 miles of operation, whichever occurs first. GM also will reimburse owners who in the past may have paid to have the condition corrected during the time and mileage limits of the special policy, provided they present proper receipts to their dealer.

The earlier special policy, announced in January, 1988, covered certain cars built between 1982 and 1985.

# # # # #

Based on materials provided by CAS, I called Chevrolet about the power steering on my 1984 Cavalier; they told me to take it to a dealer who would advise me. After the dealer checked with GM, there was no question re payment. Had I not approached GM with the CAS information, I feel certain I would have paid the $429 repair cost.

A. Pattaxox
Kensington, Maryland

I spoke with GM and the dealership at least 6 times about the loss of power steering on my 1985 Chevrolet Cavalier. Until I wrote to CAS and found out about the secret warranty, I was getting nowhere. After I got the straight scoop, GM paid for a new rack and pinion power steering system at a cost of $650.

T. Pulcini
Lyndhurst, New Jersey

DEALERS NOT TOLD: THE $1 BILLION FORD PICKUP PAINT GOOF

When secret warranties are really big, manufacturers often do not even tell their dealers about them. If dealers don't know about the secret warranty, obviously, fewer consumers will get reimbursed. Here consumers have to complain so loudly that they get beyond the dealers and reach a factory representative. In effect, those dealers oblivious to the secret warranty act as filters preventing customers from contacting the manufacturer's field representatives charged with implementing the adjustment policy.

One of the most costly secret warranties ever occurred on 1985–92 F-series pickups, *America's best selling vehicle*, which outsold any other car or truck *for the past ten years*. Ford sold nearly five million pickups with defective paint. Because Ford skipped a primer layer beginning in 1985, paint peels off these trucks like skin from a bad sunburn.

While the paint peel condition is seen mostly on blue, silver, and grey vehicles, it is not limited to these colors. These three colors peel with the greatest frequency because they are among the five most popular paint colors and low pigment, metallic colors such as these are most likely to experience a bond breakdown between paint layers. Ultraviolet light (sunlight) contributes to the condition. Ford skimped in its paint process and omitted the traditional acrylic urethane primer layers commonly applied between the anti-corrosion primer and colorcoat layers. It is the exclusion of this intermediate primer layer from the paint process which is largely to blame for the paint peel defect.

What made Ford's conduct particularly egregious was the fact that the manufacturer continued to produce F-series trucks using the questionable paint process. While inundating consumers with advertising proclaiming that "Quality is Job 1," Ford simultaneously knowingly produced and sold trucks with a costly, latent paint defect to unsuspecting consumers. Paint facility upgrades costing $350 million were not completed at Ford's Wayne, Michigan and Norfolk, Virginia truck plants until mid-year 1993. Other Ford truck plants had paint facility upgrades somewhat earlier.

A Ford whistle-blower revealed that Ford management said the paint peel defect on its pickups could cost Ford a whopping one billion dollars if consumers got their trucks repainted by Ford. To shift this cost to consumers, Ford did not tell dealers about the secret warranty but alerted only its regional representatives. Only particularly aggressive consumers were able to get to these representatives and get their entire truck repainted free.

Despite the lack of notification to its dealers or its customers, Ford issued a Technical Service Bulletin (#91-18-1) that clearly established its trucks had defective paint (see pp. 37). One reason

SEPTEMBER 5, 1991　　　　　**BULLETIN NO. 91-18**

TECHNICAL
SERVICE
BULLETIN

FEATURED IN THIS BULLETIN:

● Comprehensive Exterior Paint Repair
Procedure . . . . .1985-86 CAPRI, LTD, MARQUIS;
1985-87 LYNX; 1985-89 XR4Tl; 1985-90
BRONCO II, C SERIES; 1985-91
CL-CLT-9000 SERIES; 1985-92
BRONCO, CONTINENTAL, COUGAR,
CROWN VICTORIA, ECONOLINE,
ESCORT, F & B SERIES,
F-150-350 SERIES, GRAND MARQUIS,
L SERIES, MARK VII, MUSTANG,
RANGER, TEMPO, THUNDERBIRD,
TOPAZ, TOWN CAR; 1986
CARGO SERIES; 1986-92 AEROSTAR,
SABLE, TAURUS; 1988 F-47; 1988-89
SCORPIO; 1988-92 F SUPER DUTY,
FESTIVA, TRACER; 1989-92 PROBE;
1991 EXPLORER

PARTNERS IN CUSTOMER SATISFACTION

FORD: 1985-86 LTD
1985-92 CROWN VICTORIA, ESCORT, MUSTANG, TEMPO, THUNDERBIRD
1986-92 TAURUS
1988-92 FESTIVA
1989-92 PROBE

LINCOLN-MERCURY: 1985-86 CAPRI, MARQUIS
1985-87 LYNX
1985-92 CONTINENTAL, COUGAR, GRAND MARQUIS, MARK VII, TOPAZ, TOWN CAR
1986-92 SABLE
1988-92 TRACER

MERKUR: 1985-89 XR4TI
1988-89 SCORPIO

LIGHT TRUCK: 1985-90 BRONCO II
1985-92 BRONCO, ECONOLINE, F-150-350 SERIES, RANGER
1986-92 AEROSTAR
1988 F-47
1988-92 F SUPER DUTY
1991 EXPLORER

MEDIUM/HEAVY TRUCK: 1985-90 C SERIES
1985-91 CL-CLT-9000 SERIES
1985-92 F & B SERIES, L SERIES
1986 CARGO SERIES

(B) PAINT-EXTERIOR COLOR PEELING FROM ULTRA VIOLET LIGHT

Paint may be damaged because of ultra violet light absorption through the color coat. This damage will cause the top coat to peel to the E-coat primer.

If service is required, use the following procedure to correct the concerns.

1. Wash the vehicle with soap and water.

2. Verify topcoat adhesion by applying a 2 inch wide masking tape strip on all body panels above and below the beltline on each panel.

   a. Pull the tape up quickly.

   b. Inspect the adhesive side of the tape for paint removal.

NOTE: IF PAINT WAS REMOVED DURING THE TAPE TEST, THE ENTIRE PANEL SHOULD BE STRIPPED AND REFINISHED AS NECESSARY.

Ford issued this TSB was so that paint peel repairs performed under Ford's secret paint warranty would be done right the first time by Ford dealers. In this document, Ford ingeniously buried the problem of paint peel due to ultraviolet light among nine other less significant paint concerns. Ford also lumped together all vehicles to which the TSB applied, rather than identifying individual model lines with any particular paint concern among the ten outlined therein.

After CAS exposed this secret warranty in July 1992, Ford sent pickup owners an evasive letter asking them to tell Ford if they had any problems with their truck. Most owners thought the letter was a typical survey and ignored it (See letter on page 40.) Ford should have told owners that F-series pickups were prone to paint peel and to bring them in for free repair. Because they did not do so, Ford paint peel continued to be a secret warranty.

REGIONAL SECRET WARRANTY:
FORD RACK AND PINION STEERING

Another type of secret warranty is regional: Consumers in some states are notified about a defect and free repairs for it, but consumers in other states are not. This type of notification is particularly common for failures related to cold weather, humid weather, corrosion, and other geographical or climatic factors. The trouble is that consumers in non-notification states often have the same failure. Many consumers move from state to state, vacation in other states or have a particularly severe winter or hot summer that causes the failure. Finally, the regional lines defined by the manufacturer are often arbitrary. For example, in the mid-1980s, Ford Motor Company had an extended warranty on the defective rack and pinion steering system in 5.9 million 1978-83 full- and mid-size Fords, but notified only 900,000 owners in 17 northern "cold weather states." The 5 million owners in the 33 other states were not notified of the extended warranty and thus were subject to a

What is a Secret Warranty?

Thomas J. Wagner
Vice President-General Manager
Ford Parts & Service Division

Ross H. Roberts
Vice President-General Manager
Ford Division

August 19, 1992

Sample A Sample
123 Main Street
Anytown, USA 12345

Dear Mr. Sample:

On behalf of Ford Motor Company, we want to thank you for owning a 1989 Ford F-Series pickup truck. Whether or not your vehicle is still under warranty, if you are experiencing any problem with your truck or have experienced any in the past, please complete and mail the attached postage-paid reply card. Upon receipt of the card, our owner relations personnel will contact you within five working days and we will make every effort to respond to your requests. Also use the postcard if you seek general information.

We were recently recognized for six consecutive years of total truck sales leadership. We could not have achieved this goal if it were not for you...our valued customer. We are dedicated to providing you with the best product quality and ownership experience.

We sincerely appreciate your purchase of our product, and look forward to keeping you as an F-Series owner for years to come.

Sincerely,

FORD MOTOR COMPANY
CUSTOMER ASSISTANCE CENTER
P.O. BOX 43304
DETROIT, MI 48243

SAMPLE A. SAMPLE
123 MAIN STREET
ANYTOWN USA 12345

1FTHXR61KAAPP990-CDP
9999999

Ford Motor Company is committed to providing you with the best product quality and ownership experience. Of course, normal maintenance and wear and tear items are the responsibility of the owner. Your total satisfaction is our number-one priority. Please let us know if you should require assistance.

ASSISTANCE REQUESTED

☐ Service ☐ Engine ☐ Transmission ☐ Brakes
☐ Interior ☐ Body ☐ Paint (e.g. peeling)
☐ Other (explain below)

GENERAL INFORMATION

☐ Warranty ☐ New Vehicle Product Information
☐ Other (explain below)

Comments: _____

Comments: _____

The phone number where Ford Motor Company can contact you:
Daytime: (_____) _____   Evening: (_____) _____
Would you prefer to be contacted ☐ Daytime ☐ Evening ☐ No preference
Preferred Servicing Dealer _____ City/State _____

BUSINESS REPLY MAIL
FIRST-CLASS MAIL   PERMIT NO. 368   DETROIT, MI

POSTAGE WILL BE PAID BY ADDRESSEE

NO POSTAGE
NECESSARY
IF MAILED
IN THE
UNITED STATES

FORD MOTOR COMPANY
PO BOX 43384
DETROIT MI 48243-9915

secret warranty. Ford maintained that its policy was adequate because the problem was caused by cold weather which thickened the power steering fluid and placed extra stress on the steering system. Yet Ford's policy did not include some of the nation's coldest states such as Massachusetts, Pennsylvania, Ohio and Connecticut. Ford even cut New York in two, claiming that lower New York did not get cold in the winter. Complaints to CAS demonstrated that this defect occurred throughout the United States.

Freemont Broughman of Wurtland, Kentucky never received notice from Ford of the rack and pinion secret warranty on his 1978 Ford Fairmont because he lived in the "warm weather" state of Kentucky. In February 1984, the steering went out at 58,000 miles during one of Kentucky's not-so-warm winters. Ford refused to pay for the repair. Mr. Broughman got the Ford secret warranty letter from CAS and took Ford to small claims court where the judge ordered Ford to replace the rack and pinion steering for free. (See Ford's letter on page 43.)

GOODWILL ASSISTANCE DISGUISE:
JAPANESE AUTO MAKERS EXCEL

Some manufacturers disguise the existence of their secret warranties using code words in their bulletins such as "check for availability of goodwill assistance." This is particularly the case for Japanese auto companies that appear to associate a stigma with admitting to a mistake.

Even in the Toyota Camry pulsating brake secret warranty discussed above, which resulted in a $100 million class action settlement, the Toyota Warranty Bulletin on the defect listed the VIN range covering 400,000 affected cars and told dealers to "Contact your district service manager for consideration of goodwill assistance for repairs to the vehicle beyond these warranty guidelines." There was no examination of the vehicle or any other

J P King
Manager
Service Engineering Office
Ford Parts and Service Division

Ford Motor Company
3000 Schaefer Road
P.O. Box 1904
Dearborn, Michigan 48121

October, 1983

To: Selected Ford and Lincoln-Mercury Dealers

Subject: Owner Notification Programs M24 and M25 - Ford-Manufactured
Power Rack and Pinion Steering Gear Assembly on Certain 1978
Through 1983-Model Vehicles (Fairmont, Mustang, Thunderbird,
Granada, LTD, Zephyr, Capri, XR-7, Cougar, Marquis and
Continental)

The purpose of this letter is to advise you of Owner Notification Programs
M24 and M25 that are applicable only to those subject vehicles registered
in 17 northern cold-climate states. Complete technical and administrative
instructions (Attachment I) and a copy of the letter (Attachment II) that
will be sent to affected owners residing in those states are provided for
your information in the event you receive owner inquiries regarding the
programs.

We have found that a temporary reduction in power steering assist may occur
on some of the subject vehicles when first started cold. This is the result
of internal valve bore wear of the power steering gear housing and is more
evident in cold temperatures. The wear condition primarily causes an initial
start-up delay in full power assist, not a sudden and unexpected loss of power
assist. Once the vehicle is warmed-up, full power steering assist is restored
and the system will function normally.

Owner Notification Program M24 provides to owners of involved vehicles who
reside in 17 northern cold-climate states no-charge repair coverage of the
Ford-manufactured power rack and pinion steering gear assembly if the housing
valve bore wear condition occurs within five years from the vehicle in-service
date or 50,000 miles of operation, whichever comes first. Reimbursement will
be provided under Owner Notification Program M25 for prior owner-paid repairs
performed to correct the condition within the five year/50,000 mile limitation.

Specifics of the programs are as follows:

Vehicles Involved: The programs involve certain 1978 through early 1983-
                          model Ford passenger cars equipped with the Ford-manu-
                          factured power rack and pinion steering assembly. For
                          specific vehicle information, please refer to the
                          technical and administrative instructions (Attachment I)

What is a Secret Warranty?

Owners Involved:
- Owners residing in the following 17 eligible states: Alaska, Colorado, Idaho, Iowa, Maine, Michigan, Minnesota, Montana, Nebraska, New Hampshire, New York (northern section only), North Dakota, South Dakota, Utah, Vermont, Wisconsin and Wyoming. See the "Owner Notification" portion of Attachment I for specific areas in the state of New York where owners will be notified.

- Owners residing in the remaining 33 states (including a portion of New York) who possess vehicles similar to those involved in these programs are not eligible and will not be notified of these programs.

Components Covered:
- Ford-manufactured power rack and pinion steering gear assembly.

- The TRW power rack and pinion steering gear assembly is not involved in these programs. The TRW gear assembly is a two piece assembly and has a bolt-on iron control valve (pinion) housing.

- Coverage is not provided for the repair or replacement of steering gear tie rods, tie rod ends, bellows and the power steering pump, fittings, hoses and clamps beyond the new vehicle warranty. These components are not affected by the internal valve bore wear of the power steering gear housing. The repair of external power steering system fluid leakage also is not covered.

Repair Coverage:
- Ford will pay the replacement cost (parts and labor) of the Ford-manufactured power rack and pinion steering gear assembly when required as a result of internal valve bore wear of the power steering gear housing within five years from the vehicle in-service date or 50,000 miles of operation, whichever comes first.

Reimbursement:
- Owners will be reimbursed for prior Ford-manufactured power rack and pinion steering gear assembly replacement/repair costs incurred within five years from their vehicle's in-service date or 50,000 miles of operation, whichever comes first.

- Reimbursement will include the deductible amount owners may have paid under Ford's Major Components Coverage (applicable only to Continental), Ford's Extended Service Plan (ESP) or any similar plan in effect on their vehicles.

- Owners are to request reimbursement from dealerships by May 31, 1984. Dealerships must submit claims for owner reimbursement requests on separate warranty claim Forms 1863, either mailed or through the Direct Warranty Entry System, by July 31, 1984.

- 3 -

Your service personnel may perform the repairs provided under the provisions of Owner Notification Program M24 on involved vehicles registered
in the 17 eligible states including the designated northern section of
New York. Your service manager, however, must obtain authorization from
your Ford Parts and Service Division District Office prior to performing
the repairs. Further information on this matter is included in the
technical and administrative instructions. Your service personnel are
also asked to prepare claims for eligible owner reimbursement requests
within the provisions of Owner Notification Program M25.

Mailings to owners of affected vehicles who reside in the 17 eligible
states will be made in phases starting early in October, 1983. Subse-
quent mailings will be made as quickly as possible without jeopardizing
parts availability. In the interim, this package should be provided to
your appropriate parts and service personnel for review and retention
until required.

Please assure that your sales and service personnel are familiar with the
details of this program in order that they may respond to owner inquiries.

Your cooperation in the administration of Owner Notification Programs M24
and M25 is appreciated.

Sincerely,

J. P. King
Service Engineering Office Manager

Attachments

owner specific consideration required for a true goodwill adjustment. All that was done was to check to see if the car fell within the VIN range and repair approval was automatic.

In September 1991, Honda issued a Service Bulletin on 1989–90 Civics that cited "an unusual amount of wear on the inside edges of the front tires" that was due to the front toe being out of adjustment. According to the bulletin, Honda was willing to pay for realignment and for a pro rata replacement of the front tires up through 36,000 miles but the bulletin noted this "requires prior DSM authorization." The bulletin also went on to state: "Any repair performed after warranty expiration may be eligible for goodwill consideration by the District Service Manager." However, the dealer authorization necessary consisted of verifying the VIN through the regional office. There was no review of repair records, purchase history, or vehicle inspection by Honda representatives as would be the case with a genuine goodwill adjustment.

The following information was provided on the TSB:

ABSTRACT OF HONDA TECHNICAL SERVICE
BULLETIN
Model: 1989–90 CIVIC
Applicable To: All
Bulletin Number: 90–030
Issue Date: September 21, 1990
FRONT TIRE WEAR
SYMPTOM
An unusual amount of wear on the inside edges of the front tires.
PROBABLE CAUSE
The front tire is out of adjustment.
CORRECTIVE ACTION
Set the front toe to 3 mm toe-in using the procedure in

section 18 of the service manual. Check the rear toe and adjust if necessary.

WARRANTY CLAIM INFORMATION

In warranty: The normal warranty applies.

Out-of-warranty: Any repair performed after warranty expiration may be eligible for goodwill consideration by the District Service Manager. You must request consideration, and get the DSM's decision, before starting work.

Tire Replacement Information—Honda will, on a pro-rata basis, pay for front tires worn due to misadjustment of the alignment at the factory. For the first 15,000 miles, Honda will pay 100% for new tires. Mounting and balancing will be paid up to 36,000 miles.

NOTE: Requires prior DSM authorization.

Service Bulletins from Japanese manufacturers consistently use this code language. For example, Acura had a major problem with its high tech automatic power seat. On its luxury 1989–90 Legends, a computer chip was supposed to memorize the preferred position for its driver. The brainy seat developed amnesia and could not remember the position. The bulletin below relating to this problem states "Any repair performed after warranty expiration may be eligible for goodwill consideration by the District Service Manager."

The TSB said, in part:

ABSTRACT OF ACURA TECHNICAL SERVICE BULLETIN

Year: 1989–90

Model: LEGEND

Vin Application: All

Bulletin No.: 92–015

Issue Date: June 22, 1992

DRIVER'S POWER SEAT MEMORY LOSES POSITION
SYMPTOM

The power seat memory does not recall the original positions, or the memorized positions are completely lost.

PROBABLE CAUSE

The power seat memory stores extra pulses whenever the ignition switch is turned on or off. These extra pulses alter the stored seat positions.

CORRECTIVE ACTION

Replace the power seat control unit with the appropriate updated unit listed under PARTS INFORMATION.

WARRANTY CLAIM INFORMATION

In warranty: The normal warranty applies.

Out of warranty: Any repair performed after warranty expiration may be eligible for goodwill consideration by the District Service Manager. You must request consideration by the District Service Manager. You must request consideration, and get the DSM's decision, before starting work.

EXPANSION OF
FACTORY WARRANTY: GM TIRE WEAR

Some manufacturers use secret warranty programs to cover parts and service that are not covered by express factory warranties, such as brake pads, tires, and batteries. Usually these items are considered to be maintenance items which are not covered by any warranty. To the extent they are covered, the consumer must go to another manufacturer, such as Goodyear, that made the part to have it replaced under the terms of the applicable tire or part warranty.

In 1985–86, General Motors made a goof at the factory that affected six million cars and trucks including most Buicks, Oldsmobiles, Chevrolets and Pontiacs. The vehicles were built with alignment problems that caused excessive tire wear and cupping on the non-drive axle. In 1986, GM sent bulletins to dealers to replace severely worn tires up to 12 months/12,000 miles, perform free alignments and install axle "shim" kits to correct the problem so that it would not reoccur. But since tiremakers—not auto companies—warranty tires, most consumers did not complain to GM and never learned of the secret warranty.

CAS received hundreds of complaints from consumers about this defect. Many reported that they just kept replacing tires because the underlying alignment problem was never fixed. Wayne Orel of Lake Arrowhead, California said he had to replace eight front tires in 23,000 miles on his 1985 Chevrolet Astro van. Richard Vandermade of Valencia, California got eighteen free tires and six free alignments because he found out about the secret warranty on his 1985 Buick LeSabre.

Once they learned of the secret warranty, many consumers got GM to pay for tire replacement beyond 12,000 miles. (See Pontiac dealer service bulletin on pages 50.)

PHASE-IN: GM DOOR HINGES
Sometimes manufacturers will implement an extended warranty (or a warranty for a part not covered by the factory warranty) immediately in some states and extend the warranty to other states at a later date. For owners not in the immediate phase-in states, this is identical to the regional secret warranty discussed above. If consumers have a failure covered by the extended warranty, they will not know about the extended warranty and are likely to pay for any related repair themselves instead of having the auto company assuming the cost. The auto companies try to justify the phase-in secret warranty by saying they are taking care of those states first where climate or some other reason makes it more likely the part will break down. In March 1992, GM put out a service bulletin (see pages 52 for an excerpt of the bulletin) in which it set forth its

Number 86-3-7   Gmo   5/86   PONTIAC MOTOR DIVISION

'86 Dealer Service Bulletin

Subject: IRREGULAR/PREMATURE TIRE WEAR - ALL SEASON TIRES

1985-86 6000 MODELS WITH 'ALL SEASON TIRES' REAR POSITION ONLY
1985-86 PARISIENNE AND GRAND PRIX/BONNEVILLE MODELS WITH 'ALL SEASON TIRES' FRONT POSITION ONLY

CONDITION:

Some 1985-1986 6000 models and some 1985-1986 Parisienne and Grand Prix/Bonneville models with original equipment all season tires ("M & S" rating on sidewall) may experience premature/irregular tire wear on non-drive axles. The wear may be identified as a cupping condition, usually on the outer shoulder of the tire. If allowed to continue, premature wear out of tread may occur.

CAUSE:

The single, most contributing cause of this type of wear, except for abusive driving, is excessive toe-in. Lack of tire rotation and low inflation pressures will also exaggerate this condition.

VEHICLES INVOLVED

1985-1986 6000 models with 'All Seasons Tires.' Rear Position Only.

1985-1996 Parisienne and Grand Prix/Bonneville models with 'All Seasons Tires.' Front Position Only.

All season tires involved are as follows:

Firestone "Supreme"   Goodyear "Vector"
General "Ameriway XT"   Uniroyal "Tiger Paw Plus"

SERVICE PROCEDURE

1. Tire wear should be inspected:

A. If only slight cupping is noticed, and the cross grooves in the tire's outside shoulder are still visible (see Figure 1), the tires should be rotated. The modified "X" pattern should be used (see Figure 2). This method will best equalize wear after a few thousand miles.

(CONTINUED)

Read, Initial & Pass On • Service Supervision   Parts   Accounting

---

86-3-7 (Page 2 of 5)

B. If the cupping or wear is severe, and/or the cross grooves in the outside shoulder are not visible, tire replacement may be necessary. Tire replacement, if required, will be made with the same brand and type tire as original equipment. These tires will be furnished on a "direct billed" basis to the dealer. Replacement tires must be obtained direct from the tire company by calling one of the following toll-free numbers:

Firestone - (216) 379-7096 (Collect)
General   - 1-800-TIRE-FIX
Goodyear - 1-800-TIRE-TBC
Uniroyal - 1-800-231-5893 (Except Texas)
           1-800-833-5906 (Texas)

Dealers must supply owner's name, vin, mileage, dealer code, tire make, size, and description (i.e., whitewall, brand name, etc.).

A maximum of two tires per vehicle will be provided on a "one time only" basis at no charge to the customer for the first 12,000 miles or 12 months.

2. A. On Parisienne and Grand Prix/Bonneville models, whether tires are replaced or rotated, front alignment must be measured. For best tire wear, reset toe to zero. Camber and caster should be set to specification.

B. On 6000 models, install Rear Axle Shim Kit, P/N 14094481, as explained in Dealer Service Bulletin 86-3-3A. This will reduce rear toe.

C. Important on all vehicles. To further help minimize tire wear, stress the importance of regular tire rotation to the owner. The modified "X" pattern at 7,500 miles is recommended. Also, point out the importance of proper inflation pressure, as listed on the tire placard on the driver's door edge.

3. Old tires must be scrapped by drilling four holes through the tire's serial number, located on the back sidewall.

Mount new tires with the yellow mark or orange label on the tire at the valve stem on the wheel. Balance and install on non-drive axle positions.

CUSTOMER REIMBURSEMENT

Claims for customer reimbursement of previously paid repairs due to the described tire wear condition, accompanied by originals of paid receipts verifying vehicle mileage, should be submitted to the consumer relations office. Vehicle mileage must be within the specified parameters to be eligible. Reimbursement amount requested should be shown as a subjet repair. Do not list parts and labor. Attach originals of customer receipts to repair order.

(CONTINUED)

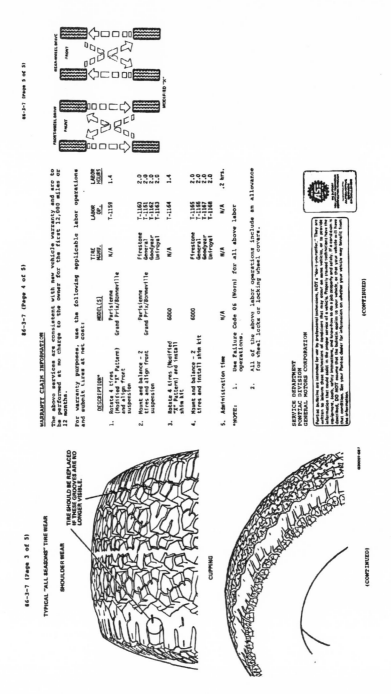

86-3-7 (Page 3 of 5)

TYPICAL "ALL SEASONS" TIRE WEAR

SHOULDER WEAR

TIRE SHOULD BE REPLACED IF THESE GROOVES ARE NO LONGER VISIBLE.

CUPPING

86-3-7 (Page 4 of 5)

WARRANTY CLAIM INFORMATION

The above services are consistent with new vehicle warranty and are to be performed at no charge to the owner for the first 12,000 miles or 12 months.

For warranty purposes, use the following applicable labor operations and submit tires at net cost:

DESCRIPTION*	MODEL(S)	TIRE MANU.	LABOR OP.	LABOR HOURS
1. Rotate 4 tires (Modified "X" Pattern) and align front suspension	Parisienne Grand Prix/Bonneville	N/A	T-1159	1.4
2. Mount and balance - 2 tires and align front suspension	Parisienne Grand Prix/Bonneville	Firestone General Goodyear Uniroyal	T-1160 T-1161 T-1162 T-1163	2.0 2.0 2.0 2.0
3. Rotate 4 tires (Modified "X" Pattern) and install shim kit	6000	N/A	T-164	1.4
4. Mount and balance -2 tires and install shim kit	6000	Firestone General Goodyear Uniroyal	T-1165 T-1166 T-1167 T-1168	2.0 2.0 2.0 2.0
5. Administration time	N/A	N/A	N/A	.2 hrs.

*NOTE:
1. Use Failure Code 06 (Worn) for all above labor operations.

2. All of the above labor operations include an allowance for wheel locks or locking wheel covers.

SERVICE DEPARTMENT
PONTIAC DIVISION
GENERAL MOTORS CORPORATION

(CONTINUED)

(CONTINUED)

86-3-7 (Page 5 of 5)

REAR-WHEEL DRIVE

FRONT

FRONT-WHEEL DRIVE

FRONT

MODIFIED "X"

What is a Secret Warranty?

Bulletin Number: 89-SM-11
Reference Number:
Publish Date: March, 1992

PONTIAC DIVISION
'89
Dealer
Service
Management
Bulletin

Subject: SPECIAL POLICY ADJUSTMENT
DOOR HINGES

1988-89 GRAND PRIX COUPE MODELS
WITH 8.7mm CONICAL PIN DOOR HINGES

General Motors has determined that certain 1988-89 Grand Prix coupes with 8.7mm conical pin door hinges have had a door hinge break while opening or closing a door. If the lower hinge breaks, the door may require more effort to close, or a popping or scraping noise might be heard. If the upper hinge breaks, the end of the door nearest the door handle may drop down, making the door difficult to reposition and close properly.

NOTICE

It's been determined that a primary cause of door hinge fractures is corrosion of the door hinge. Accordingly, the majority of vehicles experiencing this condition will be located in high corrosion areas (Canadian Maritime Provinces, New England, Great Lakes States).

As a result (and also due to limited parts availability) owner mailings will be phased out first to owners of vehicles located in high corrosion areas and then expanded to include other regions. Dealers should be certain to consider this corrosion factor when placing parts orders.

VEHICLES INVOLVED

Involved are certain 1988-89 Grand Prix coupes with 8.7mm conical pin door hinges built within the following VIN breakpoints:

Year	Plant	Beginning	Up To And Including
1988	Fairfax	JF200001	JF286357
1989	Fairfax	KF200001	KF230159

Pontiac bulletins are intended for use by professional technicians, NOT a "do-it-yourselfer." They are written to inform these technicians of conditions that may occur on some vehicles, or to provide information that could assist in the proper service of a vehicle. Properly trained technicians have the equipment, tools, safety instructions, and know-how to do a job properly and safely. If a condition is described, DO NOT assume that the bulletin applies to your vehicle, or that your vehicle will have that condition. See your Pontiac dealer for information on whether your vehicle may benefit from the information.

Read, Initial & Pass On   • Service Supervision   • Parts   • Accounting

89-SM-11 (2 of 5)

SPECIAL POLICY ADJUSTMENT

This Special Policy covers the condition described above for ten (10) years and unlimited mileage with no deductible from the date the vehicle was originally placed into service regardless of ownership. Correction at no charge to the customer will consist of replacing all door hinges in involved vehicles which experience failure of any 8.7mm single-hung door hinge. 11.3mm single-hung hinges will be used to replace the 8.7mm single-hung hinges when a failure occurs.

REIMBURSEMENT

Customer claims for reimbursement on previously paid repairs to correct a fractured door hinge are to be submitted by December 31, 1992 (the time limitation for presenting the original paid receipt may be longer depending upon the law in your state). Owners must submit original documentation that reasonably confirms the amount for unreimbursed repair expense, a description of the repair, the date of the repair and the person or entity performing the repair. Customers claims for reimbursement are to be submitted using the special "Owner Reimbursement" labor operation listed under the Claim Information Section of this bulletin. Reimbursement amounts of $300.00 or less can be processed by the dealer. If the amount exceeds $300.00 an Owner Reimbursement Form 7201-039 must be forwarded to and processed by the Zone Office. Customers from the states of Connecticut and Virginia must submit request for reimbursement directly to Pontiac Division per the owner letter.

OWNER NOTIFICATION

Owners will be notified of this campaign on their vehicles by Pontiac Division (see copy of Owner Letter included with this bulletin).

PARTS INFORMATION

Parts required to complete this campaign are to be obtained from General Motors Service Parts Operation (GMSPO). To ensure that these parts are obtained as soon as possible, they should be ordered from GMSPO on a C.I.O. order with no special instruction code, but on advise code (2).

Description	Part Number	Quantity Per Vehicle
Left Door Hinge Kit	10218446	1
Right Door Hinge Kit	10218445	1

Each door hinge kit contains 2 hinges, 4 nuts and 4 bolts.

Due to initial parts quantity restrictions, please limit the ordering of hinge kits to previous hinge fracture rates experienced by this vehicle population.

000405/92

policy of replacing, free of charge, door hinges that broke due to corrosion on its 1988–89 Grand Prix Coupes and 1988–89 Buick Regal Coupes. The factory warranty covers these door hinges for 12 months or 12,000 miles. The special policy is good for 10 years/unlimited mileage from the "date the vehicle was originally placed into service regardless of ownership." In the bulletin GM said that it would notify by mail "owners of vehicles located in high corrosion areas" first and would later notify owners in other regions. GM's reasons for notifying owners in "high corrosion areas" first was that the majority of the breakdowns would occur in these areas and because the supply of replacement parts was limited.

UNLIMITED PERIOD OF COVERAGE: SEAT BELTS

With the passage of mandatory seat belt use laws in most states, defects in seat belts have become more visible. Consumers believe, and rightly so, that seat belts should last for the life of the vehicle. Slowly but surely, manufacturers are beginning to agree. For all its models since 1987, Honda has written lifetime coverage for seat belts into its express factory warranty. For 1970-86 models, Honda has a extended warranty for seat belts as shown below.

When questioned by CAS or the media, manufacturers say they have a lifetime warranty for defects in seat belts. For example, Chrysler confirmed that it will replace defective seat belts for unlimited time and mileage. Nissan also has a lifetime seat belt warranty on its vehicles. In an interview with *The New York Times*, GM stated it would replace any defective seat belt during the useful life of a vehicle. Unlike Honda, GM has not written this policy into its express factory warranty so it remains a secret warranty and consumers must complain loudly to get defective belts replaced.

Most consumers are unaware of the lifetime seat belt warranty and pay for the repairs themselves. For example, Dominick Torrago of Anchorage, Alaska wrote:

> Are there any warranties, secret or otherwise, for seat belts? I had to replace the seat belts on my daughter's 1986 Pontiac Grand AM. The retractor portion would not retract. Both the driver and passenger side seat belts failed and needed replacement at a cost of $200.

Carol O'Malley was irate when she found that not only would she have to pay to get the seat belts replaced on her 1986 Ford Escort but that they were out of stock.

> My 1986 Ford Escort LX is only six years old and both the front seat belts are no longer operating properly. I took it to a local dealer who said the belts are not repairable and need to be replaced at a price of $125 each. When the dealer ordered the replacement belts, Ford told him this was a discontinued part which Ford would have to order from whatever vendor had made that year's seat belts.

For automatic seat belts, the cost of repair skyrockets. Lucia Smeal of Alpharette, Georgia reported she had to pay $500 to get the automatic seat belt on her 1988 Toyota Camry fixed when it stuck in one position. The part alone—the computer control—cost $400 to replace. At such high costs, consumers should leave no stone unturned to find seat belt secret warranties. (See Honda's service bulletin and news article from *The New York Time*, August 10, 1986 on pages 56–57.)

Unknown to consumers and many dealers, auto companies also offer free seat belt extenders when the original seatbelt is too short to fit around the occupant or around child seats. For example, T. Supple of Ventura, California wanted a seat belt extended for his 1988 Cadillac Eldorado. After several dealers said nothing could be done, Mr. Supple got the runaround from Cadillac:

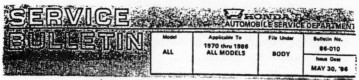

Model	Applicable To	File Under	Bulletin No.
ALL	1970 thru 1986 ALL MODELS	BODY	86-010
			Issue Date MAY 30, '86

Seat Belt Limited Warranty

Effective immediately, American Honda is providing a lifetime limited seat belt warranty to the owner of any 1970 through 1986 model year Honda automobile.

CUSTOMER NOTIFICATION

Customers will be notified of American Honda's Seat Belt Limited Warranty through advertisements appearing in many major magazines during June, July and August 1986. Copies of this Seat Belt Limited Warranty have been made available to you for your customers at your dealership. Use reorder number YO193 to obtain additional copies of this warranty.

SEAT BELT LIMITED WARRANTY

While seat belts can't eliminate all injury, they can provide a very significant level of protection when used properly. American Honda believes that seat belt use is the best method of enhancing occupant safety presently available, and that the seat belts should always be in good operating order for use by the vehicle occupants.

This warranty is given by American Honda Motor Co., Inc., 100 W. Alondra Blvd., Gardena, CA 90248-2702, a California corporation, to the owner of any 1970 through 1986 model year Honda automobile distributed by American Honda and sold through its authorized dealers in the United States, Puerto Rico and the U.S. Virgin Islands.

WARRANTY COVERAGE

American Honda will repair or replace, at its option, any factory installed seat belt that fails to function properly during normal use, free of charge for parts and labor. All parts replaced under this warranty become the property of American Honda.

TIME PERIOD

This warranty continues for the useful life of the car.

THIS WARRANTY DOES NOT COVER

• Malfunction due to misuse, alteration, abuse, accidental damage or damage resulting from a collision.

• Replacement of a properly functioning seat belt because of cosmetic reasons.

TO GET WARRANTY SERVICE

You must take your car to any authorized Honda automobile dealer in the United States, Puerto Rico or the U.S. Virgin Islands during his normal service hours.

If you can't get warranty service, or you are dissatisfied with the service or with a warranty decision, contact the nearest American Honda Zone Office listed on the back of this page.

DISCLAIMER OF CONSEQUENTIAL DAMAGES AND LIMITATIONS OF IMPLIED WARRANTIES

American Honda disclaims any responsibility for loss of time or use of the car, parts or vehicle in which the parts are installed, transportation or any other incidental or consequential damage. Any implied seat belt warranties, including the implied warranty of merchantability, are limited to the duration of this written warranty.

Some states do not allow limitations on how long an implied warranty lasts, or the exclusion or limitation of incidental or consequential damages, so the above limitations or exclusions may not apply to you.

This warranty gives you specific legal rights, and you may have other rights which vary from state to state.

(over)

ATB 357 (6405)

IMPORTANT INFORMATION FOR:

☐ General Manager   ☐ Parts Manager   ☐ Technician
☐ Service Manager   ☐ Warranty Clerk   ☐ Sales Manager

WARRANTY INFORMATION

1. Choose the appropriate operation number, flat rate time and defect code from the applicable Flat Rate Manual, or from one of the service bulletins listed below.

2. All replaced parts must be held for inspection by your DSM.

3. The Seat Belt Limited Warranty continues for the useful life of the car, and at no cost to the customer.

INDEX OF SEAT BELT RELATED SERVICE BULLETINS

Model	Bulletin Title	Bulletin No.	Issue Date
Civic	1974 Honda Civic Seat Belt Safety Recall Campaign	74-021	04-77
Accord	Guide Clip for Rear Seat Belt	82-024	09-82
All	Seat Belt Won't Retract	84-001	01-84
Accord Civic	Availability of Longer Driver's Side Seat Belt	84-060	11-84

THE NEW-YORK TIMES, SUNDAY, AUGUST 10, 1986 . A 23

G.M. Offers Free Repair of Faulty Seat Belts

By REGINALD STUART

Special to The New York Times

WASHINGTON, Aug. 9 — The General Motors Corporation, which markets 44 percent of all the cars sold in the United States, has decided to offer free repairs of defective seat belts in its cars and trucks.

The company's decision, acknowledged earlier this week, could put pressure on its competitors to match or exceed its plan in moves that could save automobile owners millions of dollars in repairs and replacement costs.

General Motors rejected lifetime warranties for seat belts, noting that it did not provide a lifetime guarantee on any of the parts or systems in its vehicles. But, in response to an inquiry, the company said, "If there are any safety-related defects in our safety belts, G.M. will correct them at no charge."

The Chrysler Corporation, the nation's third-largest automobile manufacturer, behind General Motors and the Ford Motor Company, said a lifetime warranty for seat belts "is under serious consideration."

Ford, the American Motors Corporation and Volkswagen of America said they were not considering special warranties for seat belts.

"It's the exception rather than the rule for people to get a defective belt replaced or repaired without a charge," said Clarence M. Ditlow 3d, executive director of the Washington-based Center for Highway Safety, an automobile safety consumer group that has long advocated the use of seat belts.

Mandatory Use of Seat Belts

Highway safety advocates say the move could also help increase the use of seat belts at a time when states throughout the country are under pressure from the auto industry, insurers and the Federal Government to adopt laws requiring drivers and front-seat passengers to use seat belts. To date, 27 states and the District of Columbia have such laws.

Defective seat belts and the car owners' unwillingness to pay for repairing or replacing them have been attributed in part to the failure to use seat belts, Mr. Ditlow said.

The move by General Motors comes a month after the Government's chief highway safety official said auto makers should voluntarily offer lifetime warranties as a means of assuring seat belt reliability.

Fear of Precedent Cited

The official, Diane K. Steed, administrator of the National Highway Traffic Safety Administration, recommended such a move while commenting on an announcement by the Honda Motor Company that it was offering lifetime warranties on seat belts in nearly a million Accord and Civic models. Honda acted after refusing a request by Ms. Steed that it voluntarily recall the vehicles in question.

Reluctance to offer a lifetime warranty stems in large part from the industry's fear of setting a precedent for expanding warranty coverage to other automobile parts and systems, said Alfred J. Fisher 3d, chairman of the American Seat Belt Council. "On the surface the seat belt sounds good, but how about an engine that never quits?" he asked, offering an example of the extremes to which lifetime warranties could be pursued.

In addition, Mr. Fisher said there were unresolved questions about liability in the case of accidents and how the cost of underwriting such a warranty program would be shared.

GIVE TO THE FRESH AIR FUND

Unfortunately, we are unable to offer specific advice because modification constitutes deviation from factory specifications. When a vehicle is released from the assembly plant, it has been inspected and is built to specifications that comply with government standards, as well as those established by the Cadillac Engineering Department. Changes may affect the vehicle adversely and we cannot forsee all the problems that may result. Therefore, Cadillac does not recommend modifying a vehicle after it has left the assembly plant.

> R. H.Covert
> Consumer Representative
> Customer Relations Center

Mr. Supple then wrote to CAS which sent him the GM bulletin reproduced on pages 59-60. The bulletin not only shows the existence of an extender but clearly states that it is free. After getting the bulletin, Mr. Supple wrote:

Thank you for your fast reply to my inquiry regarding seat belt extenders. We took the copy of the bulletin you sent us to the local dealer and set the whole place going. Neither the Parts nor the Service Departments had ever heard of such a thing. But they found out pretty quick. We got our extender for free.

WARRANTY POLICY CHANGE:
GM PAINT

Sometimes the auto companies will make a broad warranty policy change, make it retroactive, and fail to notify present owners who could benefit from the revised policy. Unlike a secret warranty for a specific defect, the warranty policy change provides reimbursement and free repairs for all potential factory defects covered by

Information from GM Service Parts Operations

SEATBELT ACCESSORIES

Q. What seatbelt accessories are available for GM cars and light- and medium-duty trucks?

A. The seatbelt accessories available include extenders for pregnant women and occupants whom the existing seatbelt does not accommodate, infant/child seat attachment belts for cars with door-mounted seatbelts, and dealer-installed rear-seat lap/shoulder belts.

SEATBELT EXTENDERS

Q. Do the extenders have to be permanently installed?

A. Each extender is designed for the individual user in a specific vehicle. It easily attaches to the existing belt latch, and can be removed when the user leaves the vehicle simply by unbuckling it.

Q. Where are seatbelt extenders available?

A. Extenders, as well as rear-seat lap/shoulder belts and infant/child seat attachment belts are available through any GM dealer.

Q. How much do seatbelt extenders cost?

A. The extender kits are free to owners of the vehicle.

INFANT/CHILD SEAT ATTACHMENTS

Q. Why would you need a special seatbelt to attach a child seat?

A. The safest location to place a child restraint is in the center rear-seat position. Many drivers however, choose to allow the child to ride in the front-passenger seat. In GM cars with door-mounted automatic seatbelts, a manual lap belt is usually not provided, and the automatic belts cannot be used to anchor child safety seats. For this reason, child seat attachments are needed for the front seat of these vehicles.

Q. How much do child seat attachments cost?

A. Child seat attachments are free to owners of the vehicle.

What is a Secret Warranty?

REAR-SEAT LAP/SHOULDER BELTS

Q. How long has GM offered rear-seat lap/shoulder belts as standard equipment?

A. GM began to include rear-seat lap/shoulder belts as standard equipment on selected 1987 models. The belts are now standard on all domestically produced GM cars, and are being phased in on domestic trucks and vans as technology permits.

Q. What about models that don't come equipped with rear-seat lap/shoulder belts?

A. GM offers more than 90 different retrofit kits which cover most GM vehicles on the road, including 20 different body styles and over 50 models of GM cars, trucks, and vans. Some of the kits are available for cars as far back as 1976. Although older models can only be retrofitted with black belts, as many as eleven colors are available for owners of late-model vehicles.

Q. Why don't you sell dealer-installed kits for all cars?

A. GM safety engineers have concluded that in a few models, a rear-seat lap/shoulder belt combination would not enhance the safety offered to rear-seat occupants by the lap belt alone. Ask your dealer if a dealer-installed kit is available for your car.

Q. What is in a rear-seat lap/shoulder belt kit?

A. Most kits include right- and left-passenger shoulder belts, and some include a belt for the middle seating position for color coordination.

Q. How much do rear-seat lap/shoulder belts cost?

A. The suggested retail price for most rear-seat lap/shoulder belts is $99.00 per kit, excluding installation.

If you have any comments or wish further information, please write us at:

GM Service Parts Operations
6060 West Bristol Road
Flint, MI 48554-2110

the policy, regardless of their cause. Exceedingly rare, such warranty policy changes are exceptionally valuable to the consumer who finds out about them.

In 1993 at the urging of CAS, General Motors changed its paint warranty policy to cover all factory defects, regardless of cause, to six years and unlimited mileage. GM went from having a standard paint warranty of 12–24 months and 12–24,000 miles to having the best paint warranty of any major manufacturer. While the primary defect which the policy addresses is delamination or peeling similar to that seen in Ford F-series pickups, the policy also covers paint defects such as blushing or cracking which has affected many manufacturers' vehicles in recent years.

With CAS' assistance, Raymond Rhodes of Red Hook, New York was able to get GM to repaint the rocker panels on his 1987 Chevrolet Caprice Brougham. He wrote CAS:

December 15, 1993

Dear CAS:

Thank you for the information about GM's common paint problem and a copy of the *Lemon Book*.

The information kit proved to be extremely helpful to obtain satisfactory correction by the selling dealership and duelling with the behemoth GM Corporation. Your organization assistance was effective to cutting through the corporate party line; such as the response given to the New York Attorney General Office (see copy enclosed).

A copy of your paint survey form (016), my phone notes dealing with the saga, and letter of August 11, 1993 to the Rhinebeck Chevrolet Dealership are enclosed for your data bank.

The matter was satisfactorily concluded with the owner-manager of Rhinebeck Chevrolet repainting the defective rocker panels.

What is a Secret Warranty?

During this saga, a local auto body paint expert advised the hood and trunk lids were also failing, advised of the GM paint problem, and provided a cost estimate to repaint the defective areas. I did not care to push the dealer beyond repair of the panels as the hood/trunk lids are failing in a slightly different and lesser degree than the rocker panels.

Again thanks for the information. Keep up the good work to keep the behemoth automakers responsive to their customers' needs and provide the quality and reliability expected in these expensive products.

Very truly yours,
Raymond Rhodes

(See Pontiac letter on page 63.)

SECRET WARRANTIES & WHISTLE-BLOWERS: TIP OF THE ICEBERG

CAS has publicly stated on many occasions that at any one time, there are at least 500 secret warranties in existence; a single manufacturer is likely to have dozens of secret warranties. On several occasions, whistleblowers at different car companies have had the courage to stand up for the consumer, and have provided a complete list of their company's secret warranties to CAS which made them public.

Each time this happens, and it needs to happen often, the list confirms that practice of secret warranties is rampant. CAS has obtained such lists for Ford, Nissan, Toyota and Volkswagen at one time or another. They are remarkably similar in listing the defect, the time and mileage limits, and the amount to be reimbursed to the consumer.

One of the best examples of this occurred in 1988 when a whistleblower sent CAS internal Toyota Motor Company docu-

PONTIAC DIVISION
General Motors Corporation
One Pontiac Plaza
Pontiac, Michigan 46340-2952

October 16, 1992

TO: All Pontiac Dealers

SUBJECT: Partners in Customer Satisfaction (PICS) -
Dealer Self-Authorization

Pontiac continually reviews the Warranty Management System to ensure that Warranty Administration achieves its purposes, including high levels of customer satisfaction with after sale treatment.

Following a recent review, Pontiac has decided to provide dealers authorization for cases involving <u>paint repairs</u> for vehicles up to six (6) years from date of delivery, without regard for mileage. This is a change from the current PICS dealer self-authorization which allows paint repair goodwill adjustments to be made up to 6 years/60,000 miles. Dealers who have deductible override capabilities may also waive deductibles as they see appropriate on this type of repair.

Paint repairs are only to be authorized beyond the warranty period by the Dealership <u>Service Manager</u> on a case-by-case basis as with any other goodwill policy adjustment.

Assistance should only be considered for cases involving evidence of a defect in materials or workmanship by the manufacturer. Assistance should not be considered for conditions related to wear and tear and/or lack of maintenance (such as fading, stone chips, scratches, environmental damage, etc.).

Please contact your Zone representative if you have specific questions.

Perry S. White
Director of Service/
Customer Satisfaction

ments that showed that the company had 41 specific secret warranties covering virtually every Toyota model (see *Detroit News* article August 26, 1988 on page 65.) On the list was Toyota's most costly secret warranty—pulsating brakes on 1983-87 Camrys. As discussed above, the Center for Law in the Public Interest filed a successful $100 million class action forcing Toyota to write owners about this secret warranty. Other Toyota secret warranties on the list included mufflers, transmissions, horns, paint, engine failures and rust.

March 29, 1990

Dear Center:

Thanks for your help. When the muffler failed at 27,000 miles on my 1987 Camry, the dealer told me it was only warranted for 12 months or 12,000 miles.

I called the Toyota 800# in Torrance CA and explained my trouble. They told me the same thing about the new car warranty until I mentioned having a copy of the 41 secret warranties on Toyotas, and rusting mufflers on Camrys was on the list. I was assured the list does not exist and Toyota has no secret warranties. We went the rounds again. The end result was a free muffler replacement as a "good will" gesture from Toyota. For whatever reason, I have been saved a bill of $179.00 plus tax that I wouldn't have gotten without your secret warranty list.

I'm troubled that I—armed with a little more knowledge than the usual customer—can get better treatment than the ordinary "Jane" asking for help. I am convinced that I would have gotten nowhere with Toyota without your list. Thanks again.

F. Fulmer
Tuscaloosa, AL

Toyota will bend on warranty, if you ask

By John E. Peterson
News Washington Bureau

WASHINGTON — Toyota Motor Corp. is reimbursing its American sales arm for repair claims on 41 components that are out of warranty, a company executive confirmed Thursday.

The reimbursements, made under a program described by an auto consumer activist as a "secret warranty," let dealers provide free services to customers and replace parts with above-normal defect rates, said Bob Daly, Toyota's national service operations manager.

Virtually every Toyota car, truck and van sold in the United States since the 1970s contains at least one of the 41 components, according to a 12-page Toyota document sent to The Detroit News this week. An unsigned cover letter on stationery from Toyota's Cincinnati distributor accompanied the document, and the envelope carried that office's printed address.

Daly, interviewed from the headquarters of Toyota Motor Sales USA in Torrance, Calif., confirmed the validity of the leaked document, which was dated September 1987 and labeled "Japan appeal claim processor guidelines."

He said it came from the parent company.

It lists the components by vehicle model and length of extended warranty coverage.

Please see Toyota/8A

Toyota

Auto firm bends warranty on some parts, if you ask

From page 1A

Some are as minor as cracked dashboard pads or peeling blue paint, while others are as complex as slipping automatic transmissions and engine-cylinder wear.

Problems also affect camshafts, cruise controls, catalytic converters, fuel pumps, exhaust manifolds, brakes, fuel pumps, power trains, seat backs, shock absorbers, speedometers, mufflers, universal steering joints and water pumps.

Daly said defects have been found on "only a tiny fraction" of vehicles, although he could not provide a number. Toyota sold 972,440 vehicles in this country last year.

"We have one of the highest quality ratings," Daly added. "These are not problems that occur in a broad spectrum. The 41 items on the list have nothing to do with failure rates other than in a general way."

THE NATIONAL service manager said Toyota's district offices decide whether to authorize free post-warranty repairs by dealers, who call first for approval. Toyota's current warranty runs for three years or 36,000 miles, but earlier models had shorter coverage.

A customer "generally has to complain about paying" for a component on the "high frequency of repair" list to be reimbursed, Daly acknowledged. "A dealer might point out to him that a component shouldn't have failed and offer to seek reimbursement from Toyota, but in most cases it would be up to the customer to request it," he said.

Trying to head off anticipated criticism, Daly said the policy doesn't amount to a "secret warranty" — a phrase used by consumer activists to describe an industry policy of sometimes extending warranties for buyers who complain forcefully enough.

"WE DO NOT have a secret warranty," he said. "We make a case-by-case determination under our customer satisfaction policy whether to reimburse for a repair that occurs beyond the normal warranty."

Daly suggested that the internal document might have come from "a disgruntled employee." He said it was "only an internal accounting document that shows how we get reimbursed by our parent company. It is only used long after the customer and the dealer get paid for repairs."

Toyota and most other automakers have long acknowledged paying for selected post-warranty repairs to keep customers satisfied. Dealer service bulletins outlining such arrangements have been leaked to consumer groups or the press in the past, but Toyota's list apparently is the longest ever made public.

CLARENCE DITLOW, director of the Center for Auto Safety, a public interest group in Washington, examined the list Thursday and said it "clearly constitutes a secret warranty." He added:

"What they're doing is taking care of customers who are likely to cause them image problems by reworking too loudly, while ignoring thousands of others who don't complain because they don't know a particular component of their car has a problem."

Free Toyota repairs

Toyota Motor Corp. says it will provide repair reimbursements to its U.S. sales arm for post-warranty work on the following components. The company stresses, however, that dealers will perform free repairs only on a "case-by-case" basis. Models and years are listed when available.

1. Oil filter engine damage in 1983 Corollas and Tercels.
2. Camshaft in Supras and Cressidas.
3. Catalytic converters on light trucks (models not given).
4. Cruise control (actuator accelerating) in all models, all years.
5. Dashboard pads (cracks, warping) in all models, all years.
6. Disc rotors (rust, flaking) in 1983-86 Tercels.
7. Exhaust manifolds.
8. Exhaust shields.
9. Fuel pumps (cars only), all years.
10. Fuel tank (external rust) in all models and all years.
11. Oil consumption in all years.
12. Paint peeling (blue only), trucks through 1984 models.
13. Power train-related in all 1983-86 models.
14. Rust perforation in all models through 1986.
15. Seat back, seat track (bent, warped or deformed) in 1982 Tercels.
16. Shock absorbers in some trucks.
17. Speedometer shaft sleeve (oil leak) in all models, all years.
18. Thrust washer in 1983 Celicas and some 1983 trucks.
19. Transmission front input shaft bearing (L-52 transmission only) in four 1981-83 truck models.
20. Universal steering joint for eight Tercel models, depending on year.
21. Water pumps in 1983-84 Camrys.
22. Rear wheel bearings in 1981-83 Tercels.
23. Rocker arm wear (22-R only) in 1983-84 Celicas, 1983-84 trucks.
24. Truck engines (cylinder wear).
25. Muffler corrosion (causing loud noise or separation with front pipe) in Camrys.
26. Horn terminal rust in Celicas and Corollas, depending on model.
27. Paint peeling on some 1983 Supras and some 1983-84 trucks.
28. Oil-sending unit in Celicas (1983-84 only) and in trucks, vans, Corollas, Supras and Cressidas.
29. Oil pump gaskets in Camrys.
30. Disc front brake vibration in certain Camry SV and CV models, depending on year.
31. Automatic transmission (transaxle slippage) in 1983 Camry SV, 1984 Camry CV, 1985 Corolla CE.
32. Air-conditioner compressor lock sensors in Camrys.
33. Diesel cylinder head gaskets in Camrys.
34. Lower arm bushing separation in 1984-86 Camrys.
35. Sulfur odor in 1984-86 Camrys, Tercels, Celicas.
36. Engine won't start on incline in 1985-86 Camry SV.
37. Sun roof computer in 1984-85 Cressidas.
38. Head gaskets in 1985-86 trucks and 1985 Celicas.
39. Crankshaft and pulley in vans through July 1985.
40. Oil leak in power steering gear box in all Cressidas.
41. Radiator fan motors in 1983-86 Tercels.

What is a Secret Warranty?

The Detroit News
June 26, 1990

Consumer group: Nissan is using secret warranties

By John E. Peterson
Detroit News Washington Bureau

WASHINGTON — The Center for Auto Safety, alleging Nissan has been offering illegal "secret warranties" for defective car parts, is urging a federal investigation.

The Washington-based consumer group, armed with 25 pages of internal Nissan documents, planned this morning to ask for an inquiry by the Federal Trade Commission. The group's petition stems from charges by two former Nissan employees, who allege the Japanese automaker frequently offers warranty repairs only to customers who threaten to complain to authorities.

Nissan denounced the charges.

saying they came in part from disgruntled employees. Nissan spokesman Don Spetner said the firm's "good will" in repairing some defects free of charge is being misinterpreted as a "secret warranty."

The documents, provided to The News, show the amounts Nissan paid its dealers to give free repairs to customers on a wide range of defective parts.

The Center for Auto Safety alleges Nissan's "secret warranties" covered 48 defective parts — including some related to safety — on nine of the auto firm's most popular vehicles in the 1982 through 1987 model years. The cars range from the entry-

Please see Nissan/4A

Nissan
Consumer group says firm's using secret warranties

From page 1A

level Sentra to the sporty ZX and the luxury Maxima.

"This illegal practice obviously enabled Nissan to avoid millions of dollars in expenses for across-the-board recall campaigns, in effect defrauding hundreds of thousands of American consumers," auto center Director Clarence Ditlow III said Monday. "And it endangered the motoring public by leaving hundreds of thousands of cars on the road with safety-related defects."

Ditlow noted that federal law requires manufacturers to report what they identify as above-normal repair frequencies on an item and offer to make free repairs and reimburse owners for any past expense.

Providing repairs for some but not all car owners is known as offering secret warranties because there is no public announcement of the defects and a large percentage of customers never realize they would be reimbursed for repairs. In Nissan's case, repairs were made only after customers complained about the defects.

THE DOCUMENTS submitted by the center were provided by Fred Gramcko, who was director of consumer support for Nissan Motor Corp. in the United States from 1982 to 1988, and Richard Hoffman, Nissan's U.S. director of engineering from 1979 to 1986.

Gramcko has a lawsuit pending alleging Nissan wrongfully fired him. A similar suit by Hoffman against Nissan recently was dismissed.

Nissan spokesman Spetner said company lawyers are studying the center's charges, but added "any documents supplied by Gramcko are automatically suspect." Nissan is countersuing Gramcko, alleging

breach of loyalty, breach of contract, fraud and accepting up to $350,000 in bribes from an insurance firm he hired to cover Nissan's extended warranty contracts with customers.

"We have always cooperated with all government agencies, and we will do it in this case," Spetner said. "We have a very customer-oriented approach toward any vehicle complaints, and as a result we have a liberal 'good will' policy. They're interpreting our good will policy as a 'secret warranty.' We obviously disagree."

THE ALLEGED secret-warranty repairs included safety-related items, such as fuel pumps, power steering assemblies and steering gear racks.

Some of the alleged defects are extremely costly to repair. Owners of 1985 Maximas, for example, had to spend about $1,600 to repair power steering gear racks that suddenly leaked fluid, according to documents provided to the center by Gramcko.

Gramcko, a former General Motors official, also charged that Nissan engineers "rigged" a braking test on a Nissan 280Z in 1980 in response to a National Highway Traffic Safety Administration (NHTSA) investigation into sudden acceleration involving the sports car. The test falsely persuaded NHTSA investigators that the car could be safely stopped even if the throttle were fully opened, he charged.

Gramcko, in a telephone interview Monday, charged Nissan saved "millions of dollars" by buying off consumer complaints that otherwise might have forced it to mount large-scale recall campaigns.

He charged that the alleged secret warranties covered defective parts on hundreds of thousands of Nissan cars and light trucks in the model years from 1982 to 1987.

"Most frequently, incidents that should have been disclosed to owners of affected vehicles were covered up with a secret warranty," he said. "The home office in Tokyo would say 'we recognize there's a problem with a particular part. Take care of it by buying off those who complain.' The problem was only a small percentage of customers ever got taken care of by Nissan."

Nissan complaints

Here's a list of defective parts for which Nissan reportedly offered free repairs to some customers — allegedly to keep them from complaining to federal and state regulatory agencies. The practice is called a secret warranty and it is illegal because not all customers are treated equally. The data covers various models and model years.

Pulsar - Sentra

Part	Model year
Fuel pump assembly	1983-85
Vacuum control modulator	1984-86
Rear suspension	1984-87

200SX

Part	Model year
Rear spring	1986
Front door finisher	1985

Stanza

Part	Model year
Carburetor assembly	1983
Torque converter	1984
Transmission case	1983

Stanza wagon

Part	Model year
Governor assembly	1986
Steering gear rack	1986-87

ZX

Part	Model year
Turbocharger	1986
Battery heat shield	1985-86
ATC control assembly	1983

Exhaust gas warning system 1985

Truck

Part	Model year
Cylinder block	1984
Cylinder head gasket	1982
Transmission case	1986

Maxima

Part	Model year
Drive plate assembly	1986
Muffler	1986
Alternator	1985-86
Starter	1987
Battery	1985
Head lamp	1986
Fuel level sensor	1986
Compressor assembly	1984-85
Antenna	1985-86
Torque Converter	1985-87
Transmission case	1986
Oil pump	1985
Clutch assembly	1986
Sunroof motor	1986
Steering gear	1985-87

Source: Nissan Motor Co. Center for Auto Safety and former Nissan officials Fred Gramcko and Richard Hoffman

The Detroit News July 4, 1990
Secret warranty?

Japan's Nissan Motor Co. and its U.S. affiliate paid dealers nearly $15.5 million from October 1986 to March 1987 to make special repairs on cars of customers who complained. The company calls the payouts a "goodwill" expense, but consumer activists say they constitute an illegal secret warranty that should have been available to all owners of the affected cars. Here's a list of the top ten problem parts that received unpublicized free repairs:

Model	Component	Amount paid by NMC
Sentra	Rear suspension arm assembly	$710,980
Maxima	Governor assembly	$267,759
200 SX	Front door finisher	$200,416
Maxima	Compressor assembly	$152,046
Maxima	Guide rail	$145,698
Sentra	Vacuum control modulator	$126,648
200 SX	Rear coil spring	$127,686
Maxima	Drive plate assembly	$118,432
300 ZX	Display unit	$115,521
Sentra	Fuel pump assembly	$111,360

Source: Nissan internal documents, Center for Auto Safety

In 1990, another whistleblower provided CAS documents showing that Nissan had at one time up to 48 secret warranties covering various cars and trucks. The whistleblower's assistance plus CAS' efforts in publicizing the secret warranties enabled consumers to save hundreds of thousands of dollars in these cases. (See *Detroit News* article, June 26, 1990 on page 66.)

CHAPTER 3

HOW TO FIND A SECRET WARRANTY

Until secret warranty disclosure laws are passed in every state, discovering existing secret warranties will require a lot of hard work. One will have to research dealers, libraries, federal agencies, and consumer groups to find evidence of a secret warranty. And even then, information might be so ambiguous or incomplete that one might have to apply the famous duck test—if it looks like a duck, walks like a duck, and quacks like a duck, it is a duck. Remember: If there is a common defect for which an auto company has established a policy of consumer assistance beyond the terms of the original express warranty, and has not notified individual owners, then it is a secret warranty. Even if the auto company calls it a good will program or policy adjustment, it still remains a secret warranty.

While consumers hope to find the one magical document calling itself a secret warranty, they often must settle for information that establishes individual elements of a secret warranty. Consumers must access the various sources of information on auto defects that are the first indicators of secret warranties.

BEGIN AT THE BEGINNING

* Dealer technical service bulletins (TSB's) are the single best place to begin a search for secret warranties. Every manufacturer

publishes TSB's to help dealers diagnose and repair problems on vehicles they service.

- The next best source of information is from consumer complaints and news from other owners on what auto companies did for them when they had a failure after the warranty expired or that was not covered by the warranty in the first place.
- Trade publications often run stories on widespread defects.
- Occasional articles in magazines and newspapers cover major secret warranties.
- Consumer groups collect information on secret warranties.
- State consumer agencies may require manufacturers to provide information on secret warranties.

AUTO COMPANIES

When looking for a secret warranty, start with the source—the auto company and its franchised dealer. When confronted by an angry consumer who uses the right terms and won't go away, the auto companies will often repair a defect for free. To save face, the company may claim it's doing this to keep the consumer's goodwill—not because there is a secret warranty. Who cares what the car company calls it so long as they fix your car for free.

All manufacturers keep their dealers informed through the issuance of service bulletins and shop manuals. Among the main functions of service bulletins are: to inform the dealer of new products or a revised repair procedure; to set standard procedures for the repair of persistent or widespread problems; and to specify any necessary warranty adjustments for special repairs or modifications. Under consent decrees with the Federal Trade Commission, General Motors and Volkswagen make service bulletins available to the public. For information on obtaining bulletins, call the following toll-free lines: GM at 800-551-4123 and VW at 800-544-8021. A cooperative dealer will show you any applicable bulletins on your car.

When approaching a manufacturer or dealer, use their terminology. Ask if there is a policy adjustment or good will program on your car's problem. If they say there is no program, ask if there are any service bulletins on your car's problems. At the dealer, talk to the service manager; the service writer and mechanic are not routinely informed about these programs. The best person at the manufacturer is the zone or regional representative who visits dealers and knows about secret warranties even if the dealer doesn't.

If the dealer or manufacturer is uncooperative, tell them the reason you believe there is a secret warranty. If you have a service bulletin, show them the bulletin. If you have an article, show them the article. If you know others who got their cars fixed for free for the same problem, tell them about that.

CAS wrote consumer Allen Osterling that it had received thousands of complaints on GM automatic overdrive transmission failures and believed there was a secret warranty. GM had reimbursed many consumers after the expiration of the factory warranty. Upon receiving this information, Mr. Osterling sprang into action:

> Many thanks for the assistance you gave me on claiming a warranty rebate on the automatic transmission failure in my 1984 Oldsmobile. I went to the dealer and told him I understood there was a possible secret warranty covering my expense. It was several weeks before I finally heard that I was being refunded $409.80 of my cost.
>
> A. Osterling
> Moorestown, New Jersey

Mr. Osterling is not alone in using general information on secret warranties to obtain reimbursement, as the following examples show.

I wrote to you about a cam shaft shearing off in my 1984 Honda Civic, after reading about a secret warranty in *Consumer Reports*. Within 72 hours of Honda receiving a letter from me concerning your response, and information from *Consumer Reports*, Honda offered me a settlement of $600 on a repair bill of $1200. I accepted the $600 as I no longer had the parts for them to review. I appreciate the information you sent. I now have $600 that I would not have had without your help.

S. Britton
Muskegon, Michigan

We have a 1984 Oldsmobile Cutlass Cierra with the 2.5 liter fuel injected engine. The block cracked and engine failed two weeks after we read of the secret warranty on these engines in *Consumer Reports*. We took the article into the dealer and it saved us around $1700.

R. Marohn
Madison, Wisconsin

Thanks to the information in April 1989 *Consumer Reports* I was able to get the brakes on my 1986 Toyota Camry replaced. I never received any letter concerning a problem with the brakes and it did not occur to me to complain of the vibrating sensation in the steering wheel when I applied the brakes. The report saved me at least $500.

W. Turner
Eugene, Oregon

Thank you, Center for Auto Safety, for the information you offered in the August 1991 *AAA World* magazine on secret warranties on automatic overdrive transmissions in front wheel GM cars. It was an answer to my prayers. I received a $582.39 refund from GM as a result.

M. Monteiro
East Providence, Rhode Island

AUTO DEALERS

Auto dealers who realize the value of customer relations can be your best allies in the search for the elusive secret warranty. Such dealers realize that if they treat customers fairly, they will return for more sales and service in the future. These dealers will make sure their service personnel know of major secret warranties. They will in turn inform consumers when they come in for repair of a defect covered by a secret warranty.

A good dealer will review its repair records to identify customers who have paid for repairs that are covered by a secret warranty. These dealers will then notify customers to contact the manufacturer for reimbursement. When General Motors told dealers that it would cover repair of power steering systems through five years and 50,000 miles, Sutliff Chevrolet in Harrisburg, Pennsylvania checked its files for consumers who had previously had the repair performed and alerted them that GM would likely pay for that repair bill. If the consumer had not kept a copy of the bill, as many fail to do, Sutliff sent them a copy.

The dealer who wins the Center for Auto Safety's dealer of the year award in secret warranties is Timothy Beaulieu Chevrolet Geo in Springfield, Massachusetts. This dealership knows a customer relations advantage when it sees one. The dealer took out an advertisement in the local newspaper to announce that many models were covered by three different secret warranties and to bring them in for free repair. The ad used the code phrase "Special Policy Adjustment" rather than the dreaded "secret warranty".

As the advertisement states, Beaulieu Chevrolet "will perform warranty work on all Chevrolets and GEO's sold by other dealers to help improve Chevrolet customer satisfaction." If your dealer denies there is a secret warranty, or says you are not covered by it, go to another dealer. That is what L. Gibbons of Norwich, Connecticut did when she tried to get her 1987 Oldsmobile Cutlass repainted under GM's 6-year paint warranty.

I took my car to Alderman Motor Company [an Oldsmobile dealer] and was told my car was not in the category General Motors had proposed defects on. . . . that it would cost an astronomical amount to repaint my car. [The Service Manager] said, "I can't help you get your car painted but I can sell you another car." Three days later, I had the car inspected by another Oldsmobile dealer. It took approximately three minutes for him to determine that my car did have delamination as described in the Dealer Technical Bulletin 93-T-05. He advised me I would have to pay a $100 deductible for stone chips, scratches, etc. but that they would be more than happy to repaint my car. An Oldsmobile representative confirmed that they are also more than willing to incur the expense of repainting my car for "customer satisfaction" as long as the dealer confirmed the defect.

L. Gibbons
Norwich, Connecticut

How does one find such good, consumer conscious dealers? That's the $64,000 question. Here are a few tips: Check with local consumer groups and agencies to see if they keep lists of recommended dealers who are noted for good service. The Center for the Study of Services has offices in Washington, D.C. and San Francisco and plans to open offices in other major cities; it rates dealers for customer satisfaction. If you are fortunate enough to be in one of their areas, check with them or try to find some similar local group. And once you find a good dealer, stick with it.

In addition to dealerships, repair shops can also be a source of information about secret warranties. The Sonny Hill Collision Repair Center in Kansas City, Missouri advertised in a local newspaper that owners of 1988 or newer GM vehicles might be eligible to get their paint peel problems repaired. The ad advised consumers to bring their cars in for inspection to determine if their paint problems were covered by GM's program.

Cary Emerson Curphy and Barb Holder wrote CAS about their pleasant experience with the Sonny Hill Collision Repair Center. After they complained about the paint defect on their 1989 Pontiac Grand Am, they were "told to take [their car] to Sonny Hill Body Shop . . . for an estimate." At the body shop, they made an appointment for their car to be repainted on March 15, 1993. Mr. Curphy and Ms. Holder then say: "We got the car back on 03/22/93. They [the body shop] did a wonderful job and charged us nothing! We were very impressed with their service!"

NATIONAL HIGHWAY
TRAFFIC SAFETY ADMINISTRATION

The federal agency that has the most information on secret warranties is the National Highway Traffic Safety Administration (NHTSA) which is part of the U.S. Department of Transportation

ATTENTION GM OWNERS
Reprinted from The Kansas City Star, January 12, 1993
GM dealers to pay for part of paint jobs
Automaker gives authority to make deals on cars and trucks that are affected by peeling.
If you own a 1988 or newer General Motors vehicle, you may be eligible to fix peeling paint problems on your vehicle!
In order to see if you qualify under this program please call paint repair specialists 531-9600 at the Sonny Hill Collision Repair Center and set up an appointment to have your car or truck inspected for this problem.
PEELING PAINT???
You may be entitled to have affected vehicle fixed.
(See us for details)
CALL 531-9600 for appointment
SONNY HILL
COLLISION REPAIR CENTER
"Free Estimates"
531-9600
Between Crown Center and the Plaza

(DOT). NHTSA is responsible for ordering the recall of vehicles found to have safety-related defects. To order safety recalls, NHTSA must gather vast amounts of information on auto defects ranging from consumer complaints to service bulletins to engineering reports. Hidden within this material can be found the elusive secret warranty.

NHTSA's Technical Reference Division (TRD) is the office within the agency that has all the information available from the agency on defects and secret warranties. It will advise you on the nature of the information available. It will not, however, provide any extended data by phone. In response to a written request, it can perform research on secret warranties for a small fee.

The Technical Reference Division performs manual searches in a defect investigation card catalog arranged by make/model and component. Computer searches for recalls, consumer letters, and technical bulletins also can be provided for the cost of computer time and the work of a technical information specialist. It is preferable to write to TRD, giving the details of the search requirements and authorizing a fee search; TRD will notify the requester of any additional fee upon completion of the search. In addition to its other services, TRD publishes a "Guide to The Technical Reference Division in the National Highway Traffic Safety Administration" that outlines its information systems.

The most important thing to remember when dealing with NHTSA on defects is the distinction between safety defects and economic defects. NHTSA's mission is the recall of vehicles that have safety related defects. To do this it must sift through vast amounts of information on all types of defects to identify the safety defects and recall them. NHTSA in essence throws away or disregards information on economic defects. At best it refers them to the FTC as it did with the case of collapsing Ford floor pans or the Chevette pulley bolt.

The information which NHTSA essentially disregards because it is not safety related is a gold mine for secret warranties. If the agency conducts a defect investigation, it often requires the car companies to submit all bulletins as well as information on warranty claims and complaints. Sometimes the agency never starts an investigation but accumulates a wealth of bulletins and complaints on such common problems as Chrysler's A604 Ultradrive transmission. By getting access to this information, consumers can reverse the tables on the auto company and effectively persuade them to pay for repair costs. An auto company won't want to go to small claims court to fight a consumer armed with a consumer printout of thousands of similar transmission complaints and hundreds of bulletins describing the repairs which will be covered by the manufacturer.

Here is an overview of the categories of information collected in NHTSA files:

Recall Campaigns: (A safety recall cannot be a secret warranty unless it is restricted to owners in some state like one in the "salt belt," but it may have been ordered because the auto company had a secret warranty which NHTSA discovered.) Over 170 million motor vehicles have been recalled since September 1966 (when the government began keeping records). These recalls have included vehicles made by both domestic and foreign automakers. Brief reports of each recall campaign are issued quarterly in booklet form and compiled yearly in a NHTSA publication entitled "Motor Vehicle Safety Defect Recall Campaigns." The following information is given for each campaign: manufacturer, make, model, and year of the subject vehicles, the number of vehicles affected, the defective components and the action the company took to rectify the problem. The NHTSA identification number for each campaign and the number of pages NHTSA has in the full file for each campaign are included. Copies of the Defect Recall Campaign yearly reports are sold by the Superintendent of Documents. (See

Appendix E for address.) Individual recall campaigns can be gotten from the Technical Reference Division.

Consumer Complaint Letters: The Technical Reference Division has over 250,000 consumer complaint letters on file. Those received since 1981 (about 150,000) are on a computerized database. NHTSA began this database in 1977 but periodically purges it of older complaints. The computer database is indexed by the component part involved, and also by make, year, and model of the car. NHTSA has included in this file tens of thousands of letters supplied to them by the Center for Auto Safety, which has a working knowledge of many of the trends and problems uncovered by the consumer complaints.

NHTSA will conduct a computer search of its complaint files and provide a list of complaint letters on a specific defect if the requester pays for computer time plus operator time. The average printout costs about $15 but takes up to 8 weeks to obtain. This printout will not have the name or address of the vehicle owner making the complaint. You must provide NHTSA with the make, model, and year of your vehicle plus the defect or defects on which you want a printout. The more specific your request, the cheaper the printout. Copies of individual consumer letters must then be ordered from an identification number provided for each letter on the computer printout. Both printouts and complaints can be ordered from NHTSA's Technical Reference Division. (See Appendix E.)

Defect Investigations: When safety defects of a significant nature are brought to the attention of NHTSA, the Office of Defects Investigation (ODI) frequently will undertake an investigation. About 3000 investigations have been conducted since 1968. They very rarely result in the formal finding of a defect and NHTSA-ordered recall. The manufacturers usually beat them to the punch and initiate a voluntary recall in order to avoid the onus of a formal defect finding.

NHTSA investigations are now divided into three categories with the highest being a full-scale, Formal Defect Investigation. The other two levels are a Preliminary Evaluation (PE) which is the lowest and the mid-level Engineering Analysis (EA). The Formal Investigation includes an index of all documents therein which is most useful, and a lengthy technical report when the case is closed or an initial defect determination is made. EA's and PE's do not have indexes but do have helpful "close-out" memos when the investigations are closed or moved to the next higher investigatory category. These memos summarize the information in the case and explain the enforcement action taken by ODI. Actual investigatory files are kept at ODI but public files for most cases are maintained at and may be obtained from the Technical Reference Division.

Manufacturers' Service Bulletins and Shop Manuals: Auto manufacturers keep their dealers informed through the issuance of service bulletins and shop manuals. Among the main functions of service bulletins are: to inform the dealer of new products or revised repair procedures; to set standard procedures for the repair of persistent or widespread problems; and to specify any necessary warranty adjustments for special repairs or modifications. Many times the bulletins cover safety-related problems which, theoretically, should be reported to NHTSA. There have been several cases where bulletins were issued on problems which later became subjects of recall campaigns.

Under the National Traffic and Motor Vehicle Safety Act, manufacturers must give copies of all dealer bulletins to NHTSA. Sometimes a manufacturer will provide warranty information only to its zone or regional offices, and not to its dealers, to avoid disclosure to NHTSA. Thus these zone bulletins will not normally be on file at NHTSA. NHTSA's Technical Reference Division (TRD) indexes the bulletins and can provide a computer search by year/make/model of vehicle for a specific component problem or all problems. The full set of service bulletins on microfiche is available from TRD. Since 1986, NHTSA has begun to place service bulletins on optical disks.

Shop manuals specify the manufacturer's suggested maintenance and repair procedure for a given vehicle or line of vehicles. They often contain detailed illustrations of vehicle operating systems as well as descriptions of the functions of various components. Many manufacturers sell the shop manuals to the general public. Paper copies of service bulletins and older shop manuals are held at ODI and can be requested for viewing through TRD.

In addition to demanding that the industry submit information on automobile defects, NHTSA requires all vehicle manufacturers to retain for five years all records "needed for the proper investigation, and adjudication or other disposition, of possible defects related to motor vehicle safety and instances of nonconformity to the motor vehicle safety standards and associated regulations." This includes items such as consumer complaints, test reports and warranty claims. NHTSA's address can be found in Appendix E.

FEDERAL TRADE COMMISSION

Under its broad consumer protection authority, the Federal Trade Commission (FTC) can investigate motor vehicle defects, warranty and repair practices, and illegal pricing policies or collusion by the auto industry. To avoid overlap with NHTSA's safety jurisdiction, the FTC will normally investigate only non-safety defects such as inadequate engine lubrication leading to costly engine overhauls at mileages just beyond the written warranty. If the manufacturer has a secret warranty that pays for repair costs of defects outside the written warranty, the FTC can move to require written notification to all consumers of this secret warranty.

In the 1970s and early 1980s, the FTC aggressively pursued economic auto defects and secret warranties on a case by case basis. Unfortunately, in more recent years, the FTC has all but abandoned these efforts, relying mainly on arbitration (and not disclosure) as a means of redress for consumers with warranty complaints. From the late 1970s on, the Commission reached a number of settlements with auto makers including:

Ford Piston-Scuffing and Cracked Blocks: This case represented the high point of FTC action on secret warranties. After extensive investigation, the FTC issued a formal complaint in 1978 against Ford for violating federal law by failing to inform all affected car owners of major engine design flaws in six million 1974–78 Ford vehicles. The complaint stated that Ford's advertising and promotion claims of durability and reliability were unfair and deceptive regarding the cars with major engine and transmission problems, and that secret warranty coverage for some but not all was inequitable.

The Ford engine case involved three types of defects:

1. Piston scuffing in 4-cylinder engines where elimination of the oil-feed holes that lubricate cylinder walls caused metal-to-metal contact between the pistons and cylinder walls of the engine block;
2. Camshaft/rocker arm wear in 4 and 6-cylinder engines with surface scratching or scoring which resulted from metal-to-metal contact between the camshaft and rocker arms;
3. Cracked blocks in V-8 engines where a hairline crack developed in the tappet valley wall.

This case resulted in a consent agreement (which was finalized in October, 1980 and expired in 1988) requiring Ford to mail notices to owners of vehicles covered by any adjustment program instituted from 1980 through 1988. However, the agreement did not require Ford to institute an adjustment program, just to notify consumers when it does so. The consent agreement contained the following terms:

Ford would have no more secret warranties on components that affected durability, reliability, or performance. If, in the future, a warranty were extended, ("adjustment program"), Ford would have to notify by mail all owners of affected vehicles; Ford would make generally available "technical service bulletins" (TSBs), previously distributed only to dealers, when they instituted a program regarding an engine or transmission problem that costed more than $125 to repair. In addition, because the TSBs were often written in technical language, Ford would have to furnish easy-to-read explanatory material with each TSB. Copies would be sent at low cost to consumers who request them. Subscriptions would be available for a nominal fee; and Ford would inform the public of its agreement with the FTC by setting up a toll-free phone number; through a notice in future Ford owner's manuals; through letters to owners of all 1979 and 1980 Ford vehicles; and through a three-year ad campaign in major national magazines.

Chrysler Oil Filters & Engine Damage: Under this FTC consent order, Chrysler notified owners that special strength replacement oil filters had to be used to avoid serious engine damage in 700,000 of its 1971–1980 Japanese-made cars and trucks. Replacement oil filters were leaking or bursting, causing excessive engine damage, unless they were strong enough to withstand the oil pressure used. Chrysler was ordered to send postcards to current owners of designated vehicles, describing how to avoid future oil filter leakage problems. In addition, the company had to send letters to oil filter manufacturers, providing correct information on the pressure requirements for the replacement filters.

Volkswagen Oil Filters & Diesel Engine Damage: Volkswagen was ordered to reimburse owners of 1977–81 VWs and Audis for diesel engine repairs needed because of oil filter leaks. If owners followed instructions in their manuals saying not to use wrenches to tighten replacement oil filters, the filters were more likely to leak and cause extensive engine damage. The FTC estimated that repairs would cost up to $2000. VW failed to tell owners of diesel VWs and Audis of the likelihood of oil filter leaks and that the leaks would have been less likely if the owners followed revised installation instructions. Such instructions were issued to dealers, but not to owners.

Current and past owners were reimbursed for diesel engine repairs due to any leak from a VW oil filter, and under certain conditions for damage caused when using a replacement filter sold by another company. The repairs had to have occurred prior to or within 60 days after the company mailed letters to 400,000 current owners of 1977–81 VW and Audi diesels notifying them of the problem. VW mailed the notification letters in late 1981.

Honda Rusting Fenders: American Honda Motor Company agreed to provide owners of its 1975–78 Honda Cars with replacement parts or reimbursement for repairs already completed on fenders with premature rust. About 700,000 Honda Civics and Accords were covered by this order. The rust first appeared in the form of bubbles or blisters in the paint, and soon after, holes developed in the fenders. The problem was caused by a fender design that allowed moisture and road debris, including salt, to become lodged underneath the fender.

Under the consent order, Honda had to write to owners in 24 "salt-belt" states and the District of Columbia describing the rust problem and the availability of the restitution program. The states included were Connecticut, Delaware, Illinois, Indiana, Iowa, Kansas, Kentucky, Maine, Maryland, Massachusetts, Michigan, Minnesota, Missouri, Nebraska, New Hampshire, New Jersey, New York, Ohio, Pennsylvania, Rhode Island, Vermont, Virginia, West Virginia, and Wisconsin. Owners living outside these states were also eligible for relief under the program, but had to request information from Honda.

Under the agreement, Honda was ordered to remove and

replace front fenders that showed rust within the car's first three years; offer owners a $150 cash settlement per rusted fender, or replacement of the fender; reimburse Honda owners who had paid for repairs or replacement of the front fenders if the rust occurred within the car's first three years; and provide each Honda dealership with a display poster announcing the redress program.

General Motors Transmissions, Camshafts & Diesel Engines: In 1983, the FTC reached a consent agreement with General Motors to cover failure of GM's Type THM 200 automatic transmissions; camshaft wear in the Chevrolet 305 and 350-cubic inch V-8 gasoline engines; and fuel injection system problems on the Oldsmobile 350-cubic inch diesel V-8 engines. Although the defects were found in 1976-80 models, the consent agreement covered all GM engines and transmission until its expiration in 1991.

This settlement marked the beginning of the end of FTC action on secret warranties and economic defects. Rather than requiring direct reimbursement to consumers, the consent order stipulated that GM arrange a nationwide arbitration program through the Better Business Bureau (BBB) in which consumers could seek reimbursement for repair expenses and seek a buyback of the vehicle if it could not be fixed. The best aspect of the consent agreement was that GM had to agree to arbitrate any engine or transmission failure for the life of the vehicle rather than the arbitrary 5 year/50,000 mile limit seen in the normal BBB program.

In addition, GM had to make available to the public copies of dealer service bulletins, and also advertise their availability prominently in national magazines and in owners' manuals. The obligation of GM to arbitrate under the terms of this order expired November 1991.

Saab Paint Delamination: In 1986, the FTC issued a final consent agreement with Saab-Scania of America concerning paint adhesion problems on Saab automobiles assembled at its Belgian plant. The agreement covered Saabs originally sold in the U.S. after December 31, 1977. (Saab's Belgian plant was closed after 1978.)

Consumers who owned these vehicles within their first 36 months-in-service could obtain free repairs and/or reimbursement for past repairs of paint adhesion problems that appeared within the vehicles' first 36 months-in-service. For reimbursement, repairs had to have been attempted within the vehicles' first 42 months-in-service. As an alternative to performing free repairs on cars still suffering from the paint problem, Saab was allowed to offer a cash settlement. The company's responsibility for reimbursement and free repairs was capped at $2000 per vehicle.

Saab was required to mail, within 60 days of service of the order, notice and details of the claims procedures to original purchasers of these vehicles. Saab was also obligated to send the same information to any eligible owner who, within 240 days of the initial mailing, inquired about the program.

Volkswagen Engines: In 1988, the FTC reached a consent agreement with Volkswagen of America (VWoA) settling the Commission's 1981 suit against the company for failing to disclose various oil-related engine problems in 1974–1979 Volkswagen and Audi vehicles with water-cooled gasoline engines. The main problem was defective valve stem seals that cause excessive oil consumption, resulting in engine damage due to lack of lubrication.

The order was based on the 1983 General Motors order discussed above. VWoA offered a version of the Better Business Bureau (BBB) mediation/arbitration program to all current Volkswagen and Audi owners and lessees with unresolved complaints involving internal engine components. In addition, former owners and lessees of 1974–1979 gasoline powered Volkswagens or

Audis with water-cooled engines were eligible to pursue claims in the BBB program concerning excessive oil consumption or engine damage to lack of lubrication.

VWoA also agreed to make its dealer service bulletins available to the public and to advertise the availability of the arbitration program.

Consumers can learn more about the program by calling or writing:

FTC
Consumer Education
Washington, D.C. 20850
Audi's phone number: 1-800-822-2834
VW's phone number: 1-800-822-8987

Ask for the VW Consumer Mediation/Arbitration Program fact sheet.

Jeep Eagle (Chrysler) Engines & Transmissions: In 1990, Jeep Eagle Corporation (now Chrysler) agreed to settle an FTC breach of warranty action on behalf of vehicle purchasers concerning the unsuccessful repair of automatic transmission fluid or engine oil leaks and related problems. The warranties in question involved new 1983-85 Alliances and new 1984–85 Encores and stated that "under normal use, any authorized Renault dealer in the U.S. or Canada would repair or replace any part found to be defective within a reasonable period of time."

Under the consent agreement, Jeep Eagle paid eligible consumers $40 for each repair visit beginning with the fourth visit. Through a computer search of its warranty claim files, Jeep identified vehicle owners who qualified for redress and sent them individual notice. Jeep also announced that it would redress owners who could submit documented evidence that they made four or more repair visits for a problem covered by the order.

*   *   *

Unfortunately, as seen from these examples, the FTC has all but abandoned its efforts to protect consumers from secret warranties. But the FTC's potential as a defender of the consumer can be seen in its accomplishments in the late 1970s and early 1980s.

Still, the FTC gathers valuable information on defects and secret warranties from consumers, repair shops, parts suppliers and the vehicle manufacturers. For general information on FTC files and investigations into auto defects, contact:

Bureau of Consumer Protection
Federal Trade Commission
6th & Pennsylvania Avenue NW
Washington DC 20580
(202) 326-3238

Every consumer with a secret warranty complaint should write the chairman of the FTC and ask that the Commission enforce disclosure of secret warranties.

ENVIRONMENTAL PROTECTION AGENCY

Among its many functions, the Environmental Protection Agency (EPA) oversees and regulates automobile emissions, gasoline mileage standards for automobiles, and other aspects of auto operation which affect air quality and use of fuels. The Manufacturer Operations Division of EPA has the power to investigate and recall any cars which do not meet its standards, and carries out tests of autos suspected of noncompliance at testing sites around the country. Since the EPA is always looking for defects which may cause an automobile to fail emissions standards, it has extensive files on many types of car problems, from carburetor stalling and major engine defects to excessive monoxide fumes and other toxic vapors which can enter the passenger compartment. While the most well known emission control component may be the catalyst, EPA recalls have covered items such as defective valves and fuel injection systems that cause emission levels to rise. For further information on EPA investigations, contact the Manufacturer Operations Division. (See Appendix E.)

AGENCIES THAT ENFORCE
STATE WARRANTY LAWS

Other sources of information about secret warranties are the agencies that enforce secret warranty laws in the following four states with such laws: California, Connecticut, Virginia, and Wisconsin. Even if your state does not have a secret warranty law, it is a good idea to contact one or all of these four states. If an automaker has a secret warranty in one of these states, it almost certainly will have the same secret warranty in the rest of the U.S.

The agencies in California and Wisconsin that enforce these states' secret warranty laws, the New Motor Vehicle Board and the Division of Motor Vehicles respectively, are the best source of information among the state agencies. Unlike the other secret warranty laws, the California law requires manufacturers to send to the Board copies of the notices that they send to consumers informing them of the terms of any applicable adjustment policies on their vehicles. The law also requires that the notices at the Board be "made available for public inquiries." The Wisconsin secret warranty law requires the manufacturers to notify the Wisconsin Division of Motor Vehicles of the terms of any adjustment program that they adopt.

Since the California and Wisconsin laws just recently became effective (California in January 1994 and Wisconsin in September 1992), it might take a while for their agencies to receive a significant number of notices and/or a significant amount of adjustment policy information from manufacturers. For information about any notices received by the Board and more information about California's secret warranty law, you can call or write:

New Motor Vehicle Board
1507 21st Street, Suite 330
Sacramento, CA 95814
(916) 445-1888

The Wisconsin DMV may intercede on behalf of Wisconsin residents with an automaker. For information about the Wisconsin secret warranty law, see Appendix I or contact:

Dealer Section
Wisconsin Department of Transportation
4802 Sheboygan Avenue, P.O. Box 7909
Madison, WI 53707-7909
(608) 266-1425

Consumers that call the Wisconsin DMV's 24-hour phone line (608) 266-1425 can hear a recording about the Wisconsin secret warranty law.

While the Connecticut and Virginia secret warranty laws do not require the automakers to send copies of their adjustment policy notices to state agencies, the agencies in the governments of these states charged with overseeing the secret warranty law still might be a good source of information about secret warranties. For information about the secret warranty laws in Connecticut and Virginia, contact:

Department of Consumer Protection
165 Capitol Avenue
Hartford, CT 06106
1(800) 842-2649 (toll-free)

Department of Agriculture and Consumer Services
Division of Consumer Affairs
P.O. Box 1163
Richmond, VA 23209
(804) 786-2042

‾24 AUTOMOTIVE NEWS   October 8, 1990

GM to refinish Chevrolets with paint flaking problems

General Motors said it will pay for refinishing certain 1987-90 cars and light trucks that have paint flaking problems.

As many as 323,500 vehicles exhibit paint flaking due to ultraviolet light penetrating the topcoat, degrading the primer and causing a loss of adhesion between the two surfaces, GM said.

GM said its dealers will refinish the affected vehicles or reimburse owners who present documentation that they have had such repairs made.

The adjustment programs are for about 230,000 1987-90 Chevrolet Berettas and Corsicas that are painted sapphire blue, medium sapphire blue, silver or gunmetal gray; and about 93,500 1988-89 Chevrolet S10 Blazers and S10 pickups and GMC S15 Jimmys and S15 pickups painted bright blue, dark blue or gray metallic.

The vehicles are covered for three years from the date they were put into service, regardless of mileage. Owners of 1987 and 1988 vehicles covered have until Sept. 30, 1991, to seek repairs.

GM said the problem arose from overbaking a primer with high sensitivity to ultraviolet light.

PUBLICATIONS

Periodicals: General information on a particular vehicle often can be obtained through automotive publications and magazines. Careful review of these periodicals sometimes can turn up information on secret warranties along with more general information and reviews of specific models.

Consumer Reports is the best general periodical. It tests individual vehicles in depth and publishes frequency of repair records on individual models and years based on survey reports of about 200,000 to 300,000 vehicle owners each year. The magazine will run an occasional story on a secret warranty and supports legislation to force their disclosure. Other magazines, such as *Motor Trend*, also report on particular models; note that *Motor Trend* is a consumer magazine and accepts paid advertising from the same manufacturers on which it issues reports.

For more in-depth information, individuals can turn to publications such as *Automotive News* and *Ward's Auto World*, trade journals tracking the auto industry. Trade journals will cover major secret warranties as an economic matter affecting the industry. The article on page 91 from *Automotive News* on a secret paint warranty on 1987–90 Chevrolet and GMC cars and trucks typifies the trade journals' coverage of secret warranties.

Industry Public Relations Groups: The auto and tire industries are well organized into trade associations, foundations, and councils to advance the interests of member companies through lobbying and public relation efforts. Most of these organizations provide extensive background information on the industry as well as specific reports and studies in some areas. Some even publish voluntary standards for the industry. While these groups are not likely to provide information on specific secret warranties, it never hurts for them to hear from a consumer.

The major trade groups are described below:

American Automobile Manufacturers Association (AAMA)
300 New Center Building
Detroit MI 48202
(313) 872-4311

As the domestic vehicle industry's trade association, the AAMA looks after the interests of the domestic manufacturers in Congress, the Federal agencies and state legislatures. To do this, it has offices in Detroit and Washington as well as in eight regions of the U.S. The AAMA publishes an extensive annual data book,

"Motor Vehicle Facts and Figures" as well as a comprehensive Directory of Motor Vehicle Related Associations.

Association of International Automobile Manufacturers (AIAM)
1001 19th Street, N.
Arlington VA 22209
(703) 525-7788

The AIAM is the foreign car companies' counterpart of the AAMA. It performs much the same functions as the AAMA but on a lesser scale.

Recreational Vehicle Industry Association (RVIA)
1896 Preston White Drive
Reston VA 22090
(703) 620-6003

The RVIA is the trade association of manufacturers of motor homes, travel trailers and truck campers. In addition to lobbying the Federal government, the RVIA publishes its own voluntary standards in an effort to ward off federal regulation.

CHAPTER 4

HOW TO GET THE MANUFACTURER
TO APPLY THE SECRET WARRANTY
TO YOUR CAR

I own a 1990 Plymouth Acclaim LE with the Ultradrive A604 automatic transmission. It failed me six months ago at 73,846 miles (just over the 70,000 mile written warranty). I was angry that it failed so soon after warranty and have been phoning Chrysler and writing letters to many people in their organization trying to get them to reimburse me. This has been going on since August 1992. I was determined not to stop as long as there were avenues I could take.

Approximately a week ago, when I prepared a packet of material to send into Chrysler Customer Arbitration, I received a call from Chrysler in Detroit. The caller told me they would send me the money for the parts, $809.

J. Smith
Acton, California

Every manufacturer has a system to handle consumer complaints which should be followed even though it may not work in many cases. The reason to use the system is two-fold: First, sometimes it works, as it did above, and second, complaint handling mechanisms outside the system require exhaustion of all reasonable remedies that the manufacturer provides—you must do everything within reason to get the manufacturer to apply the secret warranty to your car. The good news about the manufacturer's complaint process is that it works better for defects covered by secret warranties than for anything else.

USE THE SERVICE BULLETIN

The foremost keys to success in getting the manufacturer or dealer to apply a secret warranty to your car are to obtain the service bulletin relating to the defect and then to be persistent.

The importance of having the proper service bulletin is exemplified by A.N. Riley, who wrote to the Center for Auto Safety:

> My 1986 Chevrolet Caprice Classic had a slight vibration in the front end which got increasingly worse through 17,000 miles. The dealer was going to merely rotate the tires until I showed him your letter with Chevrolet Technical Service Bulletin 86–90–3. He then replaced the tires and aligned the front end for free. Thanks for your help.
>
> A.N. Riley
> Framingham, Massachusetts

USING PUBLIC INFORMATION

A service bulletin that spells out a secret warranty is the best information to use to get an auto company to pay for your repairs. Information on secret warranties from other sources may also be used to get the manufacturer to pay up. (Many of these sources are discussed in Chapter Three.) A little knowledge goes a long way in exercising your rights under a secret warranty. This point is demonstrated in a letter from Frieda Fulmer to the Center for Auto Safety.

> I have saved over $180 on my 1987 Camry muffler replacement that I wouldn't have gotten without reading

about your list of Toyota secret warranties. I'm troubled that armed with a little more knowledge, I can get better treatment than the ordinary Jane asking for help. I am convinced that I would have gotten nowhere with Toyota without CAS. Thanks again.

F. Fulmer
Tuscaloosa, Alabama

Sometimes consumers can capitalize on publicity about a manufacturer's secret warranty to get the benefit of the secret warranty. Dorothy Pepper of Thermal, California has a story to illustrate this point. Her 1986 Ford F150 pickup with metallic blue paint had extensive peeling with mileage less than 34,000. The dealership and its district representative turned down her March 1992 request for a free repaint job and charged her $400. On top of that, she had to drive it to a dealership in another town and wait more than three weeks for the repaint job to be finished. After hearing from a friend about CAS' June 23, 1992 petition to the Federal Trade Commission to launch an investigation of paint peeling on 1985–92 model year Ford F-series trucks, Ms. Pepper returned to the original dealer. She showed them the story about the petition from her local newspaper and asked for, and received, her $400 reimbursement.

GOOD REPAIR RECORDS
MEAN MORE MONEY IN YOUR POCKET

It is frustrating for the auto owner to learn of a manufacturer's willingness to pay for a secret warranty only to discover that the repair bills proving payment are missing. Save all your repair records and any correspondence with the auto company and the dealer. Save your maintenance records as well which show you properly maintained the vehicle—further proof that the defect could not have been caused by your lack of care. If you do not keep a log or continuous record of all periodic maintenance, save the receipts from each service performed. Saving receipts is *essential*.

SAMPLE RECORD-KEEPING SYSTEM

Repair and maintenance records should be kept in one place. A spiral notebook or a pad of paper makes a good record-keeping tool. A large envelope or folder is another good way to keep all relevant documents in one spot. Good organization comes easily if a record-keeping system is used from the time you purchase your car. Keep the records in a convenient place. If you are the kind of individual who just cannot organize anything, find an empty drawer or box and keep service receipts there.

After you've determined a defect/problem on your car is covered by a secret warranty, pull together all repair records relating to the defect/problem. These records will help you win a reimbursement for costs already incurred repairing or attempting to repair the problem. You will also want to keep track of other expenses caused by the problem such as towing charges and costs of alternate transportation. Keeping track of all of the above documents will help you to make use of the manufacturer's complaint mechanism to your benefit.

STEP # 1: GO TO THE DEALER

Always give the dealer the first chance to apply the secret warranty to your car. If possible, go to the dealership where you purchased the car. There are two reasons for this:

First, the dealer who sold you the car would like to sell you your next car, so it is likely to be more interested in seeing that you are treated fairly. The dealer can do this by applying the secret warranty in its entirety to your car or by authorizing a goodwill repair if your car is not covered by the secret warranty.

Second, the manufacturer reimburses the dealer at a rate that is usually less than the dealer would charge for regular repair work.

Hence, dealers are reluctant to provide secret warranty work for cars they did not sell.

If it is not possible to return to the original dealership, find a convenient dealership with a reputable service department. Local consumer groups and government agencies may rate or recommend local dealers.

The dealership is the first resort on almost all questions and complaints. At the dealership, ask to see the service manager. If the service manager does not make you a satisfactory offer, find out if there is a customer relations office. All but non-existent fifteen years ago, these offices exist to promote customer satisfaction. If the customer relations office does not satisfy the complaint, go to the top person at the dealership (the owner or the general manager). The top person can always overrule subordinates. Even if the top person refuses to recognize the existence of the secret warranty, or if your car is not covered by the secret warranty, he or she still may repair your car at no expense as part of a goodwill adjustment.

STEP #2 : GO TO THE MANUFACTURER

If you are not satisfied with the dealer's offer, go to the manufacturer; you will be able to tell the manufacturer that you have exhausted all possibilities with the dealer. This will help avoid one of the manufacturer's favorite ploys—referring you back to the dealer.

The manufacturer is the logical second step in the process of pursuing your rights for two reasons: First, unlike dealers, the manufacturer will always know if a certain defect in one of its own vehicles is covered by a secret warranty. And second, normally you must exhaust all remedies provided by the manufacturer in order to succeed in a case against the manufacturer in arbitration or in court.

Contact the Manufacturer's Representative

Domestic automobile manufacturers have several divisions such as the Chevrolet Motor Division of General Motors, or the Lincoln-Mercury Division of Ford Motor Company. As they get bigger, import companies have established divisions as well: Acura is a part of Honda and Lexus is a part of Toyota. Each division typically is represented in various locations across the country by a zone or district office. The zone office locations are often given in the owner's manual that accompanies each vehicle when purchased from the dealership. The zone office acts as a liaison among the main office, the dealer, and the consumer. You can ask the dealer to make an appointment with the manufacturer's representative. If the dealer refuses to do so, call the representative yourself. Local zone offices are listed in the white pages of telephone books. The manufacturer's representative will usually ask for the following basic information:

1. Owner's name, address, and phone number
2. Make, model, and year of the car
3. Selling dealer's name and location
4. Date of purchase and odometer reading (mileage)
5. Nature of problem plus attempts dealer made to repair it

The manufacturer's representative can arrange to inspect the car at either the dealership or another location convenient to the consumer. The zone offices have traveling service representatives who make regular rounds to all dealers in the zone.

In some cases, only the regional office (and not the dealer) will be notified of a secret warranty, making it particularly important to contact the local manufacturer's representative. Dealers were not informed of the $1 billion Ford F-series paint problem discussed above; consumers could only find out about the secret warranty from the regional office.

Contact the Main Office

Almost all auto manufacturers have a consumer complaint or owner relations office at their corporate headquarters or main office. Unfortunately, these offices will do little more than refer the consumer back to the zone representative. If you have already met with the zone representative, this office may put pressure on the zone office to reconsider your complaint. It is the zone office, not the main office, that actually comes out and looks at the car.

Manufacturers often have a toll-free number available for consumer complaints or "customer satisfaction." If there is a particularly pervasive problem in the news or a new crop of lemons, these lines quickly become overwhelmed. The quality of response varies from company to company.

When you can't get through on the toll-free number, call the manufacturer's regular telephone number and report your complaint. If you are not satisfied with the response from your call, put your complaint in writing (see Appendix D for addresses and telephone numbers).

Provide the main office representative with the basic information that you gave to the zone office and the objections to the way the dealer and the zone office representative handled your complaint. Be sure to take notes on all telephone conversations with the manufacturer. Keep track of the name and title of everyone with whom you talk along with the dates of the calls.

If the main office decides to review your case or otherwise intervenes, consider yourself lucky. If the main office orders further action to be taken on your case, they will usually have the zone office contact you.

Unfortunately, the manufacturer often does no more than send the consumer a form letter. When Francis Pugsley wrote to Oldsmobile about the defective paint on his 1986 Oldsmobile Delta 88, he got the royal form letter treatment:

March 24, 1993

The difficulty you referred to in your recent correspondence has been thoroughly reviewed with our New England Zone Office personnel.

Our zone office representatives have extensive training and experience in this type of situation. They are also in a position to become personally involved and obtain the information that is necessary for Oldsmobile to make a decision concerning an owner's claim.

Naturally, it is our desire to finalize all reported problems on a mutually satisfactory basis whenever possible. In your case, after careful consideration of all factors, we have concluded that our zone office personnel handled the matter in line with our policies, and we concur with the decision they have reached.

We are very sorry that we could not settle your complaint on a more satisfactory basis.

G. M. Hauser
Customer Assistance Network

Ken Klosterman of Ramsey, Minnesota had more success with the defective paint on his 1988 GMC Suburban with 100,404 miles when he wrote to GM headquarters:

I am writing in regards to a paint peeling problem on my 1988 Suburban. I took the vehicle to the local dealer who in turn contacted GMC and after a couple months of negotiations GMC agreed to pay 75%. (At first, they offered 25%, then 50% and finally 75%.) I was told this was the best offer I could get. I accepted under protest and paid my $590.78 portion.

I have since acquired a copy of a letter written to dealers authorizing them to repaint vehicles free up to 6 years. In light of this new information, I believe I am entitled to a refund of $590.78. I would appreciate any help you can give me. Thank you.

K. Klosterman
Ramsey, Minnesota

In response to this letter, Mr. Klosterman got a phone call from GM in Detroit agreeing to the full refund, which he got one week later.

NEXT STOP, ARBITRATION

After reading the January 1988 *Consumer Reports* about secret warranties on some models of 1982–86 GM automatic transmissions, I wrote to the Center for Auto Safety and got the secret warranty information on the transmission on my 1983 Buick Park Avenue that failed at 39,462 miles.

After presenting my claim to Buick, they offered me a settlement of 50% of the $1,417.80 that it cost me to fix the transmission. I refused and went to BBB arbitration. The arbitrator awarded me 100% of my claim and cited the secret warranty as one of the reasons.

E.E. Blankmeyer
Anaheim, California

With the advent of arbitration mechanisms (see complete discussion in Chapter Eight), some manufacturers will refer consumers to their own dispute resolution mechanism. Ford and Chrysler each have an arbitration board, known as the Dispute Settlement Board (Ford) and the Chrysler Customer Arbitration Board. Other companies use industry groups such as the Better Business Bureau and the Automotive Consumer Action Program (AUTOCAP). A complete listing of auto companies and their arbitration mechanisms along with a brief description of some of the major arbitration programs are found in Appendix A. If you have not received satisfactory results from your dealer, the zone office, or the main office, you may wish to contact the appropriate mechanism and submit an application to have your dispute settled by them. None of these mechanisms will hear cases which are in litigation, where the consumer no longer owns the vehicle, or where the vehicle is used for commercial purposes. Furthermore, you may not be eligible to participate in some arbitration programs because your car may have exceeded the time or mileage requirements that some arbitration programs have.

Be alert to the fact that even these arbitration groups and boards can give you the auto company-like runaround. For example, Janet Doremus was told that she did not fall within the jurisdiction of the Pennsauken, New Jersey Ford Board and that her complaint would be forwarded by them to the proper jurisdiction, South Hackensack. She then received this letter from the Hackensack Appeals Board:

> We are unable to review your case because the dealership involved does not fall within this Board's jurisdiction. We are forwarding your Customer Statement to the Ford Consumer Appeals Board at Philadelphia, P.O. Box 618, Pennsauken, New Jersey.

Once a consumer has exhausted all avenues of redress with the dealer, the zone representative, and the manufacturer, it is likely that someone along the line will admit to the secret warranty and pay your claim. If not, then the consumer will have to resort to small claims court or other remedies outside the manufacturer's system to get the secret warranty applied. In almost all cases known to the Center for Auto Safety, the consumer who can't be beaten, won't be beaten.

CHAPTER 5

FEDERAL, STATE, AND LOCAL ASSISTANCE ON SECRET WARRANTIES

Dear Center for Auto Safety:

Our office (North Carolina Attorney General) recently handled a complaint from Dr. P.J. Adler of Greenville concerning the defective steering unit in a 1984 Pontiac 6000. Initially Pontiac offered to replace the steering unit at no charge but would not pay for the labor. Apparently because Dr. Adler bitterly complained to us and our office wrote Pontiac that consumers should not pay for a manufacturing defect, Pontiac finally decided to make a "goodwill gesture" and assumed the total repair expense of parts and labor.

J.L. Grimes
Consumer Protection Section
North Carolina Department of Justice

When the manufacturer's complaint handling system does not work, the consumer can often make enough noise through aggressive and innovative complaints to get the benefit of the manufacturer's secret warranty. But a strong commitment is necessary to use these strategies successfully. Having followed the procedures in Chapters Three and Four, you should have evidence of the existence of the secret warranty and of the refusal of the dealer and the manufacturer to apply the secret warranty to your car. This evidence will make the strategies outside the manufacturer's system easier to follow and results more likely.

THE COMPLAINT LETTER

The first letter can be used as a "basic instrument" in an expanded complaint campaign. Send this basic letter to the manufacturer's chairman of the board or president with copies of the letter to others such as government agencies, consumer groups, the media, and your elected representatives. Type your letter if possible. A surprising number of complaints are ignored at this stage simply because they cannot be read, take too long to read or are misread. If you cannot type the basic letter, print or write very legibly.

GENERAL HINTS

The following suggestions will increase the effectiveness of your letter and, thus, your chances of ultimate success.

Clearly describe the defect covered by the secret warranty and any evidence that the vehicle is covered by a secret warranty. Send copies of applicable service bulletins, newspaper articles, information from the government, and materials from consumer groups and agencies. Send copies of repair bills or estimates for the defect.

Avoid an apologetic tone. If you have a legitimate complaint, simply demand action. Timidity implied in such statements as "You may think I am some sort of crank, but . . ." or, "This is the first letter like this I have ever written," does little good. On the other extreme, making yourself particularly abrasive is not to your advantage. Let your complaint carry its own weight, and try to communicate it as clearly and forcefully as you can.

Your letter should be as concise as possible. It is more effective to relate only the principal parts of an involved story. Senators and representatives, whose offices read thousands of letters, particularly appreciate brevity. On the other hand, if your predicament is complex and involved, there may be no escape from a lengthy exposition.

This one letter, along with documents supporting it, *may* resolve your complaint as happened for Franklyn Arnhoff of Charlottesville, Virginia when he wrote to Mazda's President in Japan.

But first Mr. Arnhoff wrote Mazda's Customer Relations Department in Florida and got a cold brush-off as follows:

> Dear Mr. Arnhoff:
>
> Your vehicle has exceeded the extended manufacturer's warranty. This program was instituted by Mazda as a gesture of goodwill towards its customers. There must be limits beyond which financial consideration can no longer be foreseen and this is the case here.
>
> We regret we are unable to assist you in this matter.
>
> Very truly yours,
> Customer Relations Department

Mr. Arnhoff then wrote to Mazda's President in Hiroshima saying, "The manner in which I have been treated in attempting to deal with Mazda is insulting and beneath the dignity of the company." Fourteen days after writing to Japan, Mr. Arnhoff received full reimbursement from the same customer relations office for the $733 in repairs for the defective head gasket on his Mazda 626.

Even if your letter doesn't result in success like Mr. Arnhoff's letter, it will form the basis for future action.

WHERE TO SEND THE LETTER

Address your complaint letter and mail it to the manufacturer's chairman of the board or president, certified with return receipt requested, so that you have proof it reached its destination. If the dealer and the zone office failed to help you, send copies to them as well. Addresses of company officials are included in Appendix D. Zone office addresses are usually included in the owner's manual that comes with a new car, and are often listed in local telephone directories.

Writing directly to the top may prevent many delays and avoid the necessity of writing a different letter to each person along the hierarchy—if the letter is not bumped downstairs to the customer or owner relations department. Pressure from the top may eliminate much of the runaround involving the dealer, and the central, division, and zone offices. It will also result in putting pressure upon the appropriate official—someone the top management knows can take care of the problem. People at the top are usually sensitive to problems in letters that are being sent to various federal, state, and local agencies.

SAMPLE LETTER

The following is a model letter that can be used to write to any auto company about a secret warranty.

Date

Chairman of the Board
Rickety Motors Corp.
[address]

Dear [name]:

[Identify your vehicle and, if applicable, your loyalty as a past customer and planned future purchases.]

I bought my [year] [make] [model] from [dealer's name] [address] on [date]. The vehicle identification number is [   ]. [I have been a loyal Rickety Motors customer for years. I have bought 4 of your vehicles in the last 15 years. I plan to buy 2 more cars in the near future for my 2 sons.]

The [**describe the defect: paint on the roof of the car is peeling; the car stalls frequently**]. This failure should not have occurred unless the vehicle were defective. Normally, [**name part**] last for the life of the vehicle and should not need repair.

I believe the defect on my car is so common that it is covered by an extended warranty or a special policy. [**Explain why you believe the defect is covered by a secret warranty. Discuss the evidence you have of a secret warranty such as a service bulletin or a newspaper article and enclose it along with the letter.**]

[**Describe what went wrong at the dealership.**] I took my car to [**name of dealer**]. The dealer refused to apply the extended warranty to my car because [**he said there was not an extended warranty; he said the extended warranty did not cover my vehicle's problem; etc.**]

[**Rebut the dealer's claim that your vehicle is not covered by an extended warranty.**] The dealer's decision was incorrect. My vehicle's defect is covered by a secret warranty as evidenced by [**cite whatever information you have indicating a secret warranty—e.g., technical service bulletin #XYZ, magazine or newspaper article, government agency information, or letter from consumer group.**]

I expect to have my car's defect fixed free of charge [**or whatever the secret warranty's terms call for.**] I expect to be treated fairly and to receive the benefit of your extended warranty.

Please reply within 15 days.

Sincerely,
[**Your name**]

cc: Dealer
    Zone Office
    Your attorney
    President's Office of Consumer Affairs
    Your U.S. Senators and Representative
    U.S. Senate Commerce Committee
    U.S. House Energy and Commerce Committee
    Department of Transportation
    Environmental Protection Agency
    Federal Trade Commission
    Center for Auto Safety
    Consumers Union
    Consumer Federation of America
    Action Line
    State Attorney General
    Local Attorney General
    State Senators and Representatives

Many of the above addresses can be found in this chapter. For federal government addresses, see Appendix E.

SEND COPIES OF YOUR COMPLAINT TO THE WORLD

The number of people outside the automobile industry that you advise of your secret warranty problem depends on the degree of your outrage, resources, and interest in more responsible consumer protection in the future. In general, notifying appropriate agencies and officials can only be to your advantage. James A. Hunt, owner of a 1985 Subaru with a cambelt defect, would certainly concur with this statement. He wrote to CAS:

> May 27, 1990
> Enclosed is form letter from Subaru concerning defect about which I had sent you earlier correspondence.

Subaru check was enclosed in the amount of $141.83, approximately one-half of the necessary emergency repairs.

I feel sure that only the notation on our letters to Subaru that a copy was being sent to the Center for Auto Safety impelled them to send us a check, since in an emergency situation it was impossible for us to meet all the fine points/conditions set up by them for any monetary reimbursement.

Thanks for your existence and fine work.

> Very truly yours,
> J.A. Hunt
> Bethlehem, Connecticut

Send copies of the basic letter to various organizations such as local and national consumer groups, local and state consumer protection agencies, state attorneys general, federal agencies and members of Congress. Some groups that are able to take on individual cases may give direct assistance; others may be able to give good advice on how to proceed once your complaint is mailed. A few organizations have used complaint letters to help organize a class action against the manufacturer for an unfair trade practice. Even if these agencies or groups cannot act directly on your behalf, they may send complaints on to the manufacturer requesting that the manufacturer take action. When the manufacturer receives enough complaints from consumers and organizations, it may decide to extend the secret warranty at least to those who send in the complaint letters.

INFORMING YOUR
SENATORS AND REPRESENTATIVES

Together with a cover note, send a copy of your complaint to your representative and to your senators. They were elected to represent you in Congress, so advise them of your problem getting the manufacturer to apply a secret warranty to your car. Keeping them informed has a twofold advantage. It may lead, with other letters, to increased concern in Congress, and eventually to action; it may also bring you direct results. Kelly Ann Kure wrote to her U.S. senator, Paul Simon, about the defective paint job on her 1986 Chevrolet Camaro, and GM's refusal to repair her vehicle at no cost. GM has a policy adjustment for defective paint on many of its vehicles. A few months later, Ms. Kure wrote to CAS:

> General Motors declined to help me until they were contacted by Illinois Senator, Paul Simon. His influence in this matter enabled me to win an entire paint job, a value worth $2,800!!
>
> My car is six years old and has 92,000 miles on it. I never thought I'd get a dime from GM. I cannot thank you enough for providing the public with this valuable information.
>
> K. A. Kure
> Westmont, Illinois

INFORMING OTHER GOVERNMENT OFFICIALS

President of the United States

Writing the President makes more sense than most realize—not to take up his time with your personal complaint, but because the White House will see that your letter finds its way to the most appropriate federal agency. Once the letter reaches its destination, the White House referral slip attached to it may mean more expeditious handling. In addition, all the officials who see it along the way are exposed to the problem. But most important, you have provided top officials, including the President, with an additional opportunity to learn what problems are affecting consumers and they might decide to do something about secret warranties.

Do not fear that your letter will distract the President or presidential staff from more important concerns. A part of the President's staff is charged with representing the views of consumers. It is called the Office of Consumer Affairs (OCA) and is part of the executive office of the President. The office is headed by a special assistant to the President. While the office does not have statutory authority to intercede on behalf of consumers, it does represent consumers' interests for the President and keep the federal government informed on consumer problems. The office also advises the President on policies with identifiable consumer components. It has a tiny office with a small staff, but you can help make it grow by sending copies of complaint letters, auto-related and other, to:

> President
> White House
> Washington, D.C. 20500

To help consumers solve marketplace problems, the office published the *Consumer's Resource Handbook*. This handbook is a self-help guide for consumers on how to complain about marketplace problems. It also gives consumers tips on buying cars and information on warranties and a variety of other things. The 1994 edition discusses secret warranties. Free copies are available by writing to:

> Consumer Information Center
> Pueblo, CO 81009

Federal Trade Commission
On the federal level, in addition to writing the President, send a copy of your complaint letter directly to:

Bureau of Consumer Protection
Federal Trade Commission
6th and Pennsylvania Avenue, NW
Washington, DC 20580

Also contact your regional FTC office. If consumers send enough letters complaining about secret warranties, the FTC might be persuaded to take action against a particular manufacturer's secret warranty. It might even be persuaded to return to its interpretation of statutory authority which allowed it in the late 1970s to challenge numerous secret warranties such as Ford's secret warranty on engine damage caused by piston scuffing discussed in Chapters One and Three.

National Highway Traffic Safety Administration

If the defect on your car covered by a secret warranty is safety-related, send a copy of your letter to:

Director
Office of Defects Investigation
National Highway Traffic Safety Administration
400 Seventh Street, SW
Washington, DC 20590

NHTSA sets safety standards for new cars and enforces them. It is required to investigate safety-related defects in vehicles, equipment, and tires, and to order recalls when defects are found. Consumer complaints frequently form the basis for a NHTSA recall order. In some instances, a single complaint is sufficient.

Occasionally, a manufacturer will apply a secret warranty to a car after receiving pressure from NHTSA. Eugene M. Hildegrand of Milwaukee, Wisconsin wrote to CAS of his success in getting free power steering repairs on his 1985 Oldsmobile Calais after contacting NHTSA.

I wrote to your office June, 1989 after seeing a news article concerning the power steering failure in GM cars. Based upon your reply, I contacted NHTSA. . . . NHTSA contacted the GM Zone Office, which then called the dealership October, 1989. The repair work was done at no cost to me.

E. M. Hildegrand
Milwaukee, Wisconsin

Anyone interested in getting a vehicle recall can petition the NHTSA to find that a safety-related defect exists. The petition process is initiated by your letter sent to NHTSA at the above address. To be considered a petition, the letter must:

Be written in the English language;

Have a heading that includes the word "Petition" in capital letters;

State the facts which show NHTSA that action or an order is necessary;

Give a brief description of the substance of the action or order that should be taken; and

Contain your name and address.

NHTSA must then either grant your petition and initiate the appropriate defect determination process, or deny it. The agency has 120 days to respond to your petition.

To obtain safety information from NHTSA, call its Auto Safety Hotline, toll-free. It serves the citizens of every state except Hawaii and Alaska:

Auto Safety Hotline
800-424-9393 (Outside of the Washington, D.C. area)
202-366-0123 (Washington, D.C. area)

800-424-9153 (TTY number for hearing-impaired outside Washington, D.C. area)

202-755-8919 (TTY number for hearing-impaired in Washington, D.C. area)

The Hotline serves four major purposes:

- Purchasers or owners of vehicles can verify the safety/defect/recall history of their vehicles;
- Owners can report vehicle defects to generate recalls;
- Consumers can request a variety of information from the Hotline staff including consumer educational material, equipment fact sheets, copies of safety standards and investigatory reports; and
- For vehicle and highway safety programs outside of NHTSA's jurisdiction, the Hotline can refer you to the correct agency or proper source.

Consumers who call the Hotline should be prepared to provide the year, make, and model of their vehicle and its vehicle identification number. If a safety problem is being reported, provide a brief description of the problem, the mileage, and effect the problem has on your vehicle. After calling the Hotline, you will receive a form from NHTSA to be filled out and returned. *Make sure you tell NHTSA you want your entire complaint made public. Otherwise the agency will keep it secret from consumer groups like the Center for Auto Safety. CAS and other groups rely on consumer complaints to expose secret warranties and to generate recalls.*

Environmental Protection Agency

The Environmental Protection Agency (EPA) sets emission standards for new cars and enforces them. It is required to investigate emission-related defects in vehicles and equipment and to order recalls where defects are found. Consumer complaints frequently form the basis for an EPA recall order just as they do for a NHTSA recall order. If the defect on your car covered by a secret warranty is part of the car's emission control system, write to:

Director
Office of Mobile Sources
Environmental Protection Agency
401 M Street, SW Suite 6401
Washington, D.C. 20460

Congressional Committees

You can also send a copy of your complaint letter along with a cover letter to the congressional committees responsible for consumer issues. If they receive enough letters they might put pressure on the FTC to renew their efforts to challenge secret warranties. Letters should be directed to:

Consumer Subcommittee
Committee on Commerce, Science, and Transportation
U.S. Senate
Washington, D.C. 20510

Subcommittee on Telecommunications, Consumer
    Protection, and Finance
Committee on Energy and Commerce
U.S. House of Representatives
Washington, D.C. 20515

STATE AND LOCAL AGENCIES

While you may succeed in getting help for your complaint from officials at the federal level, it is also possible to obtain individual assistance at the state and local level. The first state agency to approach on a secret warranty would be the one in charge of implementing your state's secret warranty disclosure law if your state has such a law. In Wisconsin, the Division of Motor Vehicles has the authority to intervene on behalf of a Wisconsin consumer who has a car covered by a secret warranty.

The State Attorney General and Your Local District Attorney

Send a copy of your letter to your state attorney general and to your local district attorney. Include a copy of your letter of complaint to the manufacturer. Many states' attorneys general have consumer protection offices. The attorney general's office of your state has the right to file a class action lawsuit on your behalf and on behalf of other similarly situated consumers.

State and local officials can take action only if specific laws have been broken. In a secret warranty situation, the applicable law will usually be a state's unfair and deceptive trade practices act. Although the FTC is not now challenging secret warranties, it is possible that a state attorney general will do so under the state's unfair and deceptive trade practices act if the interpretation of the act is not governed by FTC opinions.

The district attorney and the attorney general are both public prosecutors. As such, it is up to them to decide whether to prosecute after they receive a complaint. If they decide to take your case to court, charges will be pressed by the state; any conviction will usually result in a fine, an injunction, or in many states, imprisonment for the guilty company or company official.

In addition to legal recourse, the attorney general has broad powers to initiate hearings on consumer protection and safety. For instance, in 1966, the Attorney General of Iowa held hearings on unsafe design in automobiles; the hearings were instrumental in getting federal safety legislation passed. In 1987, Attorney General Bronson LaFollette of Wisconsin held hearings on problems in BBB arbitration for defective automobiles that led to improvements in the arbitration system and better decisions for consumers.

If they receive enough complaints from consumers like you or if the media exposes the secret warranty, the state attorney general or the local district attorney might negotiate on your behalf with the automaker with the secret warranty. For example, at the request of North Carolina Attorney General Mike Easley, the Ford Motor Company agreed in November 1993 to examine on a case-by-case basis the peeling paint complaints of North Carolina residents. Mr. Easley decided to act after WFMY-TV (Greensboro, NC)—working closely with CAS—exposed Ford's paint peel problem on many vehicles other than Ford's F-series trucks in three news reports. With Mr. Easley's assistance, sixty-two percent of the people that filed written complaints about Ford paint problems with the North Carolina Attorney General's office got their vehicles repainted for free.

State Boards of Consumer Affairs
and Local Consumer Protection Agencies

Another option is to send your complaint to the state board of consumer affairs or to the local consumer protection agency, if either exists. David Macali (owner of a 1986 Buick Electra) was dissatisfied with the offer of Buick's zone representative to pay $700, or half of the cost of replacement for his transmission that "failed with 12,389 miles on it, six months over the one-year warranty." He sought the assistance of the New York State Board of Consumer Affairs. Mr. Macali wrote of his saga:

> Once Buick received a letter from them [the New York State Board of Consumer Affairs], I was contacted by the Zone Rep. and offered a $500.00 "settlement," [meaning GM would pay $900 of the $1,400 replacement cost which was $200 better than GM's previous offer] telling me I was getting a great deal due to the benevolence of GM. I refused. We further negotiated and I settled the matter for

> $350.00 [meaning GM would pay $1050 of the replacement cost which was $350 better than GM's original offer of one-half of the cost of replacement], only because it would have taken me four-five months to take my claim to Small Claims Court, where I am sure I would have won my case. The New York State Board of Consumer Affairs' assistance was instrumental in getting GM to improve upon its offer.
>
> D. Macali
> Clifton Park, New York

Two of the best local consumer protection agencies in the country are New York City's Department of Consumer Affairs and Montgomery County, Maryland's Office of Consumer Affairs.

State Senators and Representatives

You can also write to your state legislators. Urge them to support the enactment of a state secret warranty law if your state does not have such a law. When you write your elected state officials, include copies of complaint letters you have written to automobile manufacturers. If you do not know the name of your state representative, check at your local library for a copy of your state's current legislative handbook, which lists the names of all representatives. Your letters can help to create a good auto consumer agency in your state if it does not already have one.

OTHER PLACES TO SEEK HELP

Local Media

The local media can be very helpful in broadcasting your secret warranty problem. Manufacturers will often respond to bad press from the local action line, newspaper, or television station and reimburse complaining customers. As discussed above, station WFMY-TV in Greensboro, NC ran three stories by reporter Greg

Hunter on Ford's secret paint warranties. Most consumers who had their vehicles highlighted in the stories got them repainted for free.

The coincidental appearance of a local TV station at his small claims court hearing with GM may have enabled Bob Burns of Santa Rosa, CA to get his 1985 GMC Suburban truck repainted for free. In response to a question on a survey put out by CAS, Mr. Burns said: "A GMC truck rep settled for an entire repaint, including stick-on mouldings, just prior to my presenting my case in court. . . . I had KGO-TV San Francisco camera personnel at my small claims court appearance as they were coincidentally doing a consumer rights series on the GM peeling paint issue. The TV camera may have made the difference although I was prepared to present a good case. I welcome contact from the staff at Center for Auto Safety to share my experience and knowledge. My court date was in Sept 93 and my Suburban is back and looking great!"

A good strategy is to announce the formation of a group to expose the secret warranty affecting your car. Even if the group consists only of you and your neighbor, a group has more power and attracts more attention than an individual. CAS serves as a clearinghouse for persons forming new organizations or developing new tactics to challenge the inequitable application of secret warranties. Send questions and success stories to us:

> Center for Auto Safety
> 2001 S Street, NW, Suite 410
> Washington, D.C. 20009

National and Local Consumer Groups

Send copies of your original letter of complaint to national and local consumer groups. Consumer groups often can file a class action against the manufacturer. In 1989, CAS helped the Center for Public Interest Law successfully sue Toyota over a secret warranty that covered up to $1800 in repair costs for pulsating brakes in over 400,000 1983–87 Camrys. To settle the class action Toyota agreed to notify all present and past owners of the problem, reimburse consumers for all repair expenses already incurred, and repair all remaining problem cars. CAS estimates the total cost to Toyota to be over $100 million, most of which would have been borne by consumers had there been no class action.

A consumer group can also function as a source of information on a secret warranty problem. When CAS received numerous consumer letters complaining of automatic transmission problems in General Motors automobiles caused by faulty transmission fluid, the group mailed out information to many thousands of frustrated consumers on how to proceed. One consumer, F.A. Rosscoe of Richmondville, New York, wrote CAS about what happened after he got CAS' information which included a copy of the GM service bulletin referred to in the form letter. Although GM had announced it would pay for a transmission overhaul regardless of mileage, GM had not been honoring its promise in many cases, including Rosscoe's. After sending GM a copy of the information on GM's own service bulletin along with the repair bill, Rosscoe received a refund for the cost of repairs with GM's full apology. In his letter to CAS, Rosscoe stated, "Once again I thank you for all your help in supplying the needed information that had to be used, even though it took almost two years to culminate in success."

The following are national consumer organizations which should be alerted to any complaints that affect large groups of consumers:

Consumers Union
101 Truman Avenue
Yonkers NY 10703

Consumers Union is a nonprofit organization, nationally recognized for its magazine, *Consumer Reports*. It does not accept advertising so its product reports and ratings are protected from the pressures of commercial incentives and advertiser interference. It often reports on secret warranties it finds, particularly in its annual report on automobiles every April.

Center for Auto Safety
2001 S Street NW, Suite 410
Washington D.C. 20009

The Center for Auto Safety (CAS) is a nonprofit public interest advocacy group organized in 1970 by Ralph Nader and Consumers Union but now independent of both. CAS bases much of its research priorities on consumer complaints. Each letter is most useful in determining patterns of defects or other problems to be investigated. CAS seeks general remedies such as vehicle recalls that will aid large numbers of similarly situated customers. This is the primary way that CAS is able to help the tens of thousands of individuals who directly seek its assistance each year or who are referred to it by Ralph Nader.

Consumer Federation of America (CFA)
1424 16th Street NW, Suite 604
Washington, DC 20036

CFA is a federation of over 500 national, state and local consumer organizations. CFA works to influence public policy formulated by Congress, the President, regulatory agencies, the courts and industry. Established in 1968, CFA describes its mission: "CFA is organized for and dedicated to advancing the consumer viewpoint through its lobbying efforts and its informational and educational services."

Although CFA does not take direct action on auto complaints, the organization is instrumental in supporting those laws and policies that protect the rights of auto consumers and efforts by other groups. CFA publishes a *Directory of State and Local Organizations* (nongovernmental), available for $5.00 from CFA.

Automobile Protection Association (APA)
The address for the APA's main office is as follows:
292 Saint Josephs Boulevard West

Montreal, Quebec

Canada H2V 2N7

The address for the Toronto branch is:

160 Pears Avenue Suite 322

Toronto, Ontario

Canada M5R 1T2

An imaginative and resourceful group of automobile owners banded together in Quebec to form the Automotive Protection Association, also known as Association pour la Protection des Automobilistes. It is an ombudsman-like organization handling "everyday grass-roots complaints of motorists, while at the same time rewarding industry personnel who are competent and honest," according to its statement of purpose. APA takes complaints on auto insurance, auto dealer-consumer problems, gas stations and auto repair gripes. It develops dossiers to back up charges and confronts industry spokespersons with problems brought to its attention. If complaints or abuses remain unsettled, the offending company often finds its problem publicized in the media and its headquarters picketed. Says APA Counselor Vladimir Cekota: "We are a small, lean and mean group while the Canadian Automobile Association (CAA) is quite large."

In addition to picketing and taking complaints, every Sunday at 8 p.m. cable viewers can tune into the Lemon Aid show, a talk show devoted solely to car talk. APA also publishes a quarterly magazine that gives information on new and used cars, information on warranties, recalls, and repairs in general. Counselors advise inquiring consumers on what cars to buy, candidly praising or criticizing performance or safety. APA handles about 100 telephone complaints a day. These calls and incoming letters serve the basis for their annual rating of automobiles.

Consumer Education and Protective Association (CEPA)

6048 Ogontz Avenue

Philadelphia, PA 19141

CEPA is an organization of consumers started in 1965 by Max Weiner, who is the education director. Through ingenious organizational devices and its achievement of an almost unbroken string of victories over those who would defraud local consumers, CEPA remains a strong and growing organization that is active in the metropolitan Philadelphia area and the part of New Jersey that is closest to Philadelphia. Both of CEPA's two branches are in Philadelphia.

CEPA's strength comes from its organizing philosophy. It will not lend its organizational backing to aid a single victimized consumer until the consumer first joins CEPA or a CEPA branch and participates in the solution of the problems common to other members. The CEPA branches in Philadelphia each cover a separate geographical area.

CEPA has considerable organizational weight to offer. When a branch decides to take action, the plan moves through several stages. CEPA first sends a letter outlining the complaint to the offending auto dealer. If the letter does not lead to a solution, the branch throws an "information" picket line in front of the dealership premises. A negotiating team accompanies the pickets and if progress is not made in the initial negotiations, the team joins the picket line. The picket continues until an agreement acceptable to CEPA is reached, often within an hour.

Reports of CEPA's activities, pictures of pickets displaying signs, photocopies of refund checks, and fraudulent or misleading contracts are published regularly in its monthly newspaper, *Consumers Voice*. *Consumers Voice* has received inquiries and subscriptions from Japan, Sweden, India, and Puerto Rico. The organization is supported in part by its members, who pay an annual fee of $15.

Consumer Action (CA)
26 Seventh Avenue
San Francisco, CA 94103

While CA does not handle individual complaints, it does give free advice to consumers on all kinds of problems.

Consumer Action gives this self-portrait:

> At Consumer Action we believe that *every* consumer should stand up for his or her rights whenever the victim of shoddy products or unfair business practices. Yet we understand all too well that a consumer alone can be nearly helpless: consumer laws are poorly enforced; individual consumer losses are often too small to justify the hiring of a lawyer; and a complaining consumer must be prepared to out-wait a runaround from the merchant that may last one year or more. Consumer Action exists to even up the odds in the battle for consumer justice in the marketplace. We are a nonprofit, community organization. Formed in 1971, our goal is to help consumers achieve greater control over their lives and a stronger voice in the decisions of government and business that affect us all. We are part of a growing, nationwide movement of consumers who believe that by working together we can correct many of our nation's problems. . . .

Motor Voters
1500 West El Camino Avenue, Suite 419
Sacramento, CA 95833-1945

Motor Voters is a nonprofit consumer organization dedicated to promoting auto safety and improving automotive business practices. The group is best known for initiating California's lemon law and its tireless efforts for air bags. Motor Voters also works for stronger safety standards for motor vehicles, better comfort and fit of safety belts, stronger bumpers, and improved disclosure of the crashworthiness of cars, vans, pickups, and minivans.

Founded in 1979 by its current president, Rosemary Shahan,

Motor Voters is an active participant in state and federal auto safety regulation, and is frequently called upon to provide testimony in legislative hearings, including providing testimony for California's recently enacted secret warranty law. The group has received major national newspaper, television, and radio coverage for its advocacy of consumer protection.

Motor Voters is an active member of the Coalition for Consumer Health and Safety, Consumer Federation of America, and National SAFE KIDS Campaign. Motor Voters is supported by member contributions and grants. Members who contribute $25 or more receive a copy of *The Car Book* by Jack Gillis and a subscription to the semi-annual newsletter, the *Motor Voter Press*.

CHAPTER 6

YOUR LEGAL RIGHTS

Consumers who know their legal rights under federal and state law are more successful in obtaining reimbursements for secret warranties. The more you know, the more persuasive you become in arguing your rights with a dealer or manufacturer. This chapter is designed to tell you what your legal rights are so you can better argue with the auto company about getting coverage under a secret warranty. And if need be, it explains your legal rights should you have to go into small claims court to get reimbursement.

Except in those states with secret warranty laws which may provide additional legal rights, a secret warranty is enforced through contracts and unfair trade practices law. Even if there is not a secret warranty on your vehicle, your legal rights discussed below may provide the grounds for reimbursement for defects and failures beyond the express written warranty that comes with every new vehicle.

YOUR WARRANTY RIGHTS

The most obvious warranty is the written factory warranty provided by the manufacturer which is a form of an express warranty. This warranty provides certain basic coverage on your vehicle for specified time periods and components. Given the trend toward longer warranties, the factory warranty today may cover components such as the powertrain for as long as 7 years and 70,000 miles. The factory warranty for the rest of the vehicle is typically 2 years and 24,000 miles. For an annual summary of factory warranty coverages each year, refer to *The Car Book* by Jack Gillis:

> *The Car Book*
> by Jack Gillis
> HarperCollins Publishers
> 10 E. 53 St.
> New York, NY 10022

Secret warranties by definition are broader than the manufacturer's written factory warranty because they cover failures not covered under the factory warranty.

The auto company creates the original written factory warranty; the auto company also creates secret warranties. In addition to the express factory warranty, your new car has other *express* warranties, *implied* warranties, and *federal-* or *state-mandated* warranties. All of these warranties may be affected by provisions of state and federal law governing how warranties are implemented. Knowing that you are protected in the following ways will encourage you, the car owner, to enforce your warranty rights.

EXPRESS WARRANTIES

The manufacturer's written warranty that comes with a new vehicle is one form of an express warranty. However, there may be other express warranties that are not in writing that can apply to the sale of both new and used cars. Like implied warranties, express warranties are also created by state law and by the representations of the manufacturer or dealer about the car.

Under state law, express warranties may be created by the seller (manufacturer or dealer) through oral promises, advertisements, brochures, or other media. Any (1) *affirmation* of fact (confirmation of the existence of a fact) or (2) *promise* made by the seller, (3) *description*, (4) *sample*, or (5) *model*, which becomes part of the "basis of the bargain" (something that serves as a foundation for the agreement), creates an express warranty—that the vehicle will conform to the affirmation, promise, description, sample or model. No specific intention to make a warranty is necessary if *any* of these factors is made part of the basis of the bargain.

Even when the seller does not use formal words such as "warrant" or "guarantee," an express warranty may still be given. But the seller's statements in which he is "puffing his wares" is not sufficient; i.e., an affirmation merely of the *value* of the vehicle (and not of *fact*) or a statement purporting to be merely the seller's opinion or commendation of the vehicle does not create a warranty. For example, the dealer who states that you are getting "a great little car" has not created an express warranty about the condition of the car. But the dealer who tells you "this car should run without any problems for at least 20,000 miles" has created an express warranty. The best way to preserve your ability to enforce such an express oral warranty is to have the dealer put any promise or warranty in writing.

IMPLIED WARRANTIES

Implied warranties are legal rights created by state law, not by the seller. To the extent they exist, implied warranties create legal rights above and beyond what is in the written warranty. Implied warranties can give consumers the right to get free repair, replacement, or a refund if the car is defective and does not work in the ordinary way a car is expected. But the consumer must take the right steps to take advantage of an implied warranty.

There are two kinds of implied warranties: an implied warranty of *merchantability* and an implied warranty of *fitness for a particular purpose*. Implied warranties come automatically with every sale even if the dealer says nothing about them and they are not in writing.

The most common implied warranty is the warranty of merchantability. This means that the car must be fit for its reasonable and ordinary uses, which include safe, efficient, and comfortable transportation from one place to another. If the car is not fit, you have a legal right to get a refund or replacement.

Implied warranties are not just applicable to the car as a whole, but to individual components as well. For example, even though your car may have 80,000 miles on it, if the transmission fails, you should be covered by the implied warranty, if the system was built to last up to 100,000 miles. Your owner's manual should indicate how long certain parts should last, even if they are not explicitly warranted to do so. This creates grounds for claim of an implied warranty.

Since a secret warranty always covers an underlying defect that causes premature failure in a vehicle, the implied warranty of merchantability should always apply to a secret warranty. In other words, when a manufacturer creates a secret warranty, it is doing nothing more than recognizing what is the consumer's right under the implied warranty.

The other implied warranty, which is less common, is the warranty of fitness for a particular purpose. This occurs when a consumer buys a vehicle for a particular purpose such as hauling a large trailer. This warranty requires the consumer to inform the salesperson of the special use and the salesperson to state that the particular model car will be good for that kind of use. When the consumer buys that model based on the salesperson's advice, an implied warranty of fitness for a particular purpose is created. If the vehicle cannot then perform the job for which it was bought, the consumer is entitled to a refund or replacement.

FEDERAL OR STATE
MANDATED WARRANTIES

Emissions Warranties

Certain components of a car, such as parts of the emission control system, may have federal-or state-mandated warranties. The period of coverage of the federal emission warranty on your car depends upon when it was made. If your vehicle was made before the 1995 model year, Section 207(a) of the Clean Air Act requires auto manufacturers to warrant for the first 5 years or 50,000 miles that vehicle emission control systems be free from defects in materials and workmanship which cause the vehicle to exceed the emission standards. Section 207(b) requires the manufacturer to warrant any component that causes the vehicle to fail an emission test during the first 24,000 miles, and any major component such as the catalyst for 50,000 miles.

If your vehicle is made in the 1995 model year and after, federal law mandates that manufacturers offer the exact same warranty in substance as if the car were built before 1995. However, Section 207(i) requires that the manufacturer's defect warranty [under Section 207(a)] and performance warranty [under Section 207(b)] last only for the first 2 years or 24,000 miles. But with respect to a catalytic converter, an electronic emissions control unit, and an onboard emissions diagnostic device, Section 207(i) requires that the manufacturer's warranty (for vehicles made after the 1994 model year) last for the first 8 years or 80,000 miles.

The purpose of this warranty is to help clean up the air and protect the consumer's pocketbook. The Clean Air Act requires that these emissions warranties appear, in some form, on the manufacturer's written warranty. For example, General Motors' 1990 limited warranty states that the vehicle was designed, built, and equipped to conform at the time of sale with applicable regulations of the U.S. Environmental Protection Agency and the California Air Resources Board; and that it is free from defects in materials and workmanship which cause the car to fail to conform with those regulations for a period of use of 50,000 miles or 5 years, whichever occurs first.

A recent case illustrates how the emissions recall and warranty provisions can work to clean the air and protect the consumer. In July, 1989 Ford had to recall 1.3 million 1985–87 cars with 4-cylinder engines with faulty throttle-body fuel injectors that violated the carbon monoxide and hydrocarbon emission standards. In addition to replacing the fuel injector, Ford had to inspect and replace for free, any catalyst and electronic engine control processor found faulty. The recall repairs saved each individual owner hundreds of dollars. Consumers who had already paid for an emission recall repair could obtain reimbursement after getting the recall notice.

The Clean Air Act makes it illegal for any manufacturer or dealer to refuse to honor a valid emission control warranty claim. If either the dealer or manufacturer refuses to make a warranty repair on the emission control system, remind them that there is a potential fine of $25,000 and then inform the Environmental Protection Agency (EPA) of the violation:

> Environmental Protection Agency
> Office of Mobile Sources
> Washington, D.C. 20460

EPA often contacts the manufacturer on behalf of the consumer to have the warranty honored.

Written Warranties
New York's Used Car Lemon Law mandates that dealers give purchasers of used cars with 36,000 miles or less a written warranty good for at least 90 days or 4,000 miles, whichever comes

first. If the used motor vehicle has more than 36,000 miles but less than 80,000 miles, the dealer has to give the consumer a written warranty for at least 60 days or 3,000 miles, whichever comes first. If the used motor vehicle has 80,000 miles or more, but no more than 100,000 miles, the dealer has to give the consumer a written warranty for at least 30 days or 1,000 miles, whichever comes first. If the used motor vehicle has over 100,000 miles or is purchased for under $1,500, dealers are not required to give consumers a written warranty.

MAGNUSON-MOSS WARRANTY ACT

In order to regulate written warranties on consumer products, Congress passed the Magnuson-Moss Warranty Act of 1975. The purpose of the Act was to make it easier for consumers to get defective cars repaired, total lemons replaced, and to successfully sue the auto companies. The Magnuson-Moss Warranty Act has several important provisions for consumers. First, it prohibits the disclaimer of implied warranties by auto companies discussed below. Second, it provides for the award of attorney fees and costs from the auto company. Third, it makes it easier to file class actions.

The Magnuson-Moss Act creates a federal right of action when a manufacturer breaches an express warranty, implied warranty, or any provision of a service contract as well as for any violation of a requirement of the Act itself. This means a consumer could sue a manufacturer for any of the above causes in state and federal court and have attorney fees and costs of the litigation paid for by the manufacturer. If you take a manufacturer to court over a secret warranty, include violation of the Magnuson-Moss Warranty Act as one claim so you can ask the court to award you all the costs of filing the lawsuit including any fee you may pay for witnesses and lawyers if you use them.

For detailed information from the Federal Trade Commission on this law, read "Warranties: There Ought To Be A Law," which can be obtained by writing:

Consumer Information Center
Pueblo, Colorado 81009

LIMITATIONS AND
DISCLAIMERS OF WARRANTIES

Manufacturers and dealers try to limit their warranty liabilities as much as possible. In the past, manufacturers attempted to disclaim outright both implied and express warranties. With a disclaimer, the manufacturer asserted that although the law may recognize an implied or an express warranty, the manufacturer would not.

Today, manufacturers can no longer freely limit and disclaim their warranty obligations. Manufacturers can disclaim and limit consumer warranty rights only if certain requirements are met.

Disclaimer of Express Warranties

If a car does not live up to the claims made by the manufacturer, the consumer can sue for breach of warranty. For example, S. Lastovich of Hibbing, Minnesota saw a Ford Motor Company television commercial showing pickup trucks dashing over rough terrain and sailing through the air. He based his purchase of a Ford four-wheel-drive truck on claims made in that commercial. After his truck was badly dented during a rough trip through mud and sand, he sued Ford for the $500 cost of repairs. Lastovich argued that Ford's ads constituted an express warranty on his pickup. Even though Ford stated in its written warranty that "there is no other express warranty on this vehicle," a jury agreed with Lastovich and ordered Ford to pay the $500 in actual damages plus $175 in costs.

S. Lastovich described the trial in a letter to the Center for Auto Safety:

> Mr. [Ken] Peterson [Lastovich's attorney] gave a very brilliant summation and the judge instructed the jury. The point of law on which their discussion rested was one of

"express warranties." Indeed, the jury ruled in effect that brochures I had read, TV ads I had seen, promises made to me by the salesperson and impressions I received from demonstrations of similar trucks as mine (on TV) influenced me to purchase the vehicle. By allowing such an excessive amount of flex in their 4-wheel drive truck frames so as to cause damage from box/cab contact, Ford was held liable to make repairs for this damage.

Some cases have held that advertisements may create express warranties even where there was no reliance by the buyer; i.e., the consumer did not have to prove he or she actually saw the ad in question, just that it was used in an effort to induce purchases of the car.

Limitations on Implied Warranties

Under the Magnuson-Moss Act, if a written warranty is given, then the implied warranties may not be disclaimed. The only limitation of an implied warranty allowed (only in "limited" but not "full" warranties) is a limit on its duration (how long the warranty lasts). The *implied* warranty cannot be limited in duration less than the *written* warranty; e.g., if you have a one-year *written* "limited" warranty, the *implied* warranties cannot be limited in duration to less than one year. Such limitation must be "conscionable," which means that it cannot be extremely unfair or harsh. Federal law also requires such limitation to be "set forth in clear and unmistakable language and prominently displayed on the face of the warranty."

Most manufacturers do limit the duration of the *implied* warranties to the duration of the *written* warranty. This means that when the *written* warranty expires after, say, 24,000 miles or 24 months, the *implied* warranties expire along with it. But many auto companies now have powertrain warranties up to 7 years, so consumers should argue that their implied warranties cannot be limited to terms less than the length of the powertrain warranty, or 7 years.

There is one important requirement on limitations of implied warranties under the Magnuson-Moss Act that may help a consumer who takes his or her secret warranty case to court: the "conscionability" argument. Usually an "unconscionable" act is one that is totally unfair or harsh to one party, or is made in bad faith. If the court agrees that the consumer, as a new car buyer, has been "unconscionably" treated by the manufacturer's warranty provisions, it may declare the warranty limitations "unconscionable" and therefore of no validity. Thus, if the dealer refuses to repair a substantial defect that exists after the written warranty has expired, the consumer should claim in court that the manufacturer has breached the implied warranty and any limitation of the implied warranty was "unconscionable."

State law under the Uniform Commercial Code (UCC), which has been adopted by all states except Louisiana, requires that a valid disclaimer of an implied warranty of *merchantability* must actually mention the word "merchantability." If the merchantability disclaimer is in writing, as it usually is in auto warranties, it must be conspicuous or visible to the average reader. A valid disclaimer of an implied warranty of *fitness* must be in writing and must be conspicuous. A disclaimer of all implied warranties of *fitness* is valid if it states, for example, that "there are no warranties which extend beyond the description on the face hereof." But this alone could not validly disclaim the implied warranty of *merchantability* because it does not mention the word "merchantability."

A seller can also disclaim the implied warranty of *merchantability* by simply adding the words "as is" or "with all faults" to the sales contract. Watch out for this tactic when buying a used car. Some jurisdictions, such as the District of Columbia and Maryland, forbid a car to be sold "as is" until it is six years old or has 60,000 miles on it.

Even when a manufacturer has attempted to limit the duration of an implied warranty, implied warranty rights are still good if you bought the car in a state which does not allow any limitations on the duration of implied warranties on consumer goods. These states are Maine, Maryland, Massachusetts, Vermont, West Virginia, and the District of Columbia, which have specifically modified their state statutes or laws so that implied warranties on consumer goods cannot be limited to a specific time period. Further, Connecticut, Kansas, and Mississippi do not allow implied warranties on consumer goods to be limited in most cases. More states are modifying their laws in this manner, so check with your state attorney general or local consumer group or agency to see whether your state has joined the above list.

LIMITATIONS ON REMEDIES

Manufacturers and dealers try to limit not only their warranty liabilities and obligations, but the consumer's rights to a remedy. A remedy is a legal tool a consumer can use for the redress of a complaint. One remedy usually limited by auto manufacturers is the right to incidental or consequential damages such as hotel bills when your car breaks down.

State law (the Uniform Commercial Code or UCC) protects the consumer from "unconscionable" limitations or exclusions on consequential damages. The UCC Section 2-719 provides that a "limitation of consequential damages for injury to the person in the case of consumer goods is prima facie unconscionable, but limitation of damages where the loss is commercial is not." Thus, if a consumer loses a week's pay because the defective car is being repaired, the manufacturer may be able to avoid liability if it excluded consequential damages.

Just as a consumer can argue that a limitation on the duration of an implied warranty is unconscionable, the same argument can apply to disclaimer of consequential damages. Public policy and state law is moving in this direction. Those states that preclude limitation on the duration of implied warranties usually also allow consumers to recover consequential damages. Many state lemon laws permit the recovery of consequential damages; consumers should cite the lemon law as an argument for permitting the recovery of consequential damages.

STATUTE OF LIMITATIONS

Even if your car is covered by an implied or express warranty under state law, the statute of limitations (SoL) may bar your claim. This is particularly likely to happen in secret warranties that may cover cars years after they are sold. Under the SoL, after a certain number of years have elapsed since the purchase date of the vehicle (usually four based on the UCC), you are precluded from pursuing your claim of breach of implied or express warranty.

However, the SoL can be overcome in many cases by arguing that the discovery rule should apply. The discovery rule is a legal concept that "tolls" (suspends) the SoL if it was impossible to discover the problem for which the suit is being brought within the SoL time period. For example, owners of GM vehicles suffering from paint delamination cannot know of the latent paint defect until the paint literally starts peeling/flaking off of their vehicles. If the peeling paint starts after the SoL, you can argue the discovery rule should apply in your case.

Another argument that sometimes can be used to overcome the SoL is that of equitable estoppel. When applying this concept, the court will not allow the manufacturer to rely on the SoL to bar your claim if it feels that considerations of justice and fairness require such a result.

For example, suppose the hood latches on automakers' vehicles corrode excessively when the vehicles are driven in states where salt is used frequently on the roads to melt ice and snow. The automaker institutes a secret warranty under which it will replace rusting hood latches up to 4 years or 40,000 miles. An owner of one of the automaker's vehicles who lives in Florida visits his aunt in Connecticut each winter. Three years after buying his car, he notices that its hood latch is starting to rust. He takes it in to his dealer, tells him he visits Connecticut each winter, and asks if he can get his latch replaced for free even though the factory warranty (1 year or 12,000 miles) has already expired. The dealer says that there is no adjustment policy on hood latches.

Refusing to take no for an answer, the consumer contacts the manufacturer, relays the same information to it, and receives the same negative response. Two years later, the hood latch rusts so badly that it breaks. The consumer sues the manufacturer to recover the cost of replacing his hood latch. The manufacturer claims that the consumer's claim is barred by the 4 year statute of limitations. In response, the consumer should argue that the manufacturer should be estopped from relying on the statute of limitation to bar his claim. He should argue that it would not be fair to allow the manufacturer to rely on the statute of limitations since only the manufacturer knew that the hood latches on its vehicles corrode excessively in cold weather states. Of course, he should also argue that he should recover since he took the vehicle in for repair while it was still covered by the adjustment policy.

HOW TO ENFORCE YOUR LEGAL RIGHTS ON SECRET WARRANTIES

When a car is defective and needs repair, begin with the manufacturer's complaint handling procedures, described in Chapter Three. If you have exhausted the manufacturer's complaint handling mechanism and the manufacturer still refuses to extend the secret warranty to your vehicle, don't give up. Sue the manufacturer in small claims court (if your claim is small enough) or in the regular courts. See Chapter Nine for detailed information on how to use small claims court.

Once a consumer with a good secret warranty claim files suit, the manufacturer often gives up, knowing that consumers nearly always win in court. For example, Fabian Wimble of Venice, Florida was able to recover the cost of repairing the power steering in his 1982 Pontiac 6000 only after suing GM in small claims court. Once sued, GM offered to settle, and Mr. Wimble accepted. (Despite the settlement, Mr. Wimble did not cancel the court hearing and later received a default final judgment against GM to cover the same repairs.) Mr. Wimble wrote to CAS: "I would like to thank you very much for your help in this matter. General Motors couldn't have cared less—until they received notice of Small Claims Court hearing!" Mr. Wimble was able to receive reimbursement from GM even though the secret warranty on his car's power steering had expired three months before he got it repaired.

Even if the manufacturer refuses to make a satisfactory offer of settlement and continues to fight a consumer's claim for repairs at no cost, courts usually hold for the consumer in valid secret warranty cases. For example, Elizabeth Nelson of Boxford, Massachusetts was able to recover the cost of repairing the power steering on her 1983 Chevrolet Cavalier. She wrote to CAS: "After trying to deal directly with Detroit, then via BBB [Better Business Bureau], I finally filed a claim in small claims court. At this point Chevrolet offered to settle for 50%. I refused. Judge ruled in my favor; dealer ordered to repay us in full! Your help was what kept me going all the way to small claims court. Keep up the good work!"

When Gary Bohon got Ford's infamous delaminating paint on his 1990 F150 pickup, he went to see attorney Dale Irwin of Kansas City after he had been turned down by Ford. Knowing that Ford had a secret warranty on the defect, Mr. Irwin filed suit against Ford in Jackson County, Missouri Circuit Court. Rather than face Mr. Bohon in court, Ford settled by giving Mr. Bohon a brand new 1992 F150 in exchange for the 1990 and paid all the attorney fees.

DECEPTIVE TRADE PRACTICES: IN THE FUTURE FOR SECRET WARRANTIES

Deceptive trade practice statutes (also called consumer protection acts) prohibit fraudulent or misleading trade practices. These laws allow state attorneys general to obtain injunctions to stop deceptive acts. Consumers may also have a private cause of action under the statutes as well: most statutes allow consumers to recover actual damages and punitive damages. And just as important, UCC defenses, such as disclaimers of warranties or limitations of remedies, are not usually available to dealers and manufacturers charged with violating a deceptive trade practice act.

Deceptive trade practice acts are particularly useful in "lemon" cases, since there are many opportunities for car dealers to mislead consumers. For example, in Texas, a breach of warranty is considered an unfair practice. Many state lemon laws define a violation of the lemon law as a deceptive trade practice. For example, Pennsylvania's lemon law states that "a violation of this act shall also be a violation of the act . . . known as the Unfair Trade Practices and Consumer Protection Law." For more information on lemon laws and lemon cars, refer to the *Lemon Book* by Ralph Nader and Clarence Ditlow:

> Lemon Book: Auto Rights
> by Ralph Nader and Clarence Ditlow
> Moyer Bell
> Kymbolde Way
> Wakefield, RI 02879
> $12.95 plus $3.50 postage

When the Federal Trade Commission was more active on secret warranties, it considered secret warranties to be unfair trade practices. While most states have not yet listed a secret warranty as one of the specific unfair trade practices in their statues, they fall under the category of a generic act that is unfair. As states pass secret warranty disclosure laws, these laws can be expected to add secret warranties to the specific lists of unfair trade practices. Such actions are essential to effective enforcement of the secret warranty laws because they may open manufacturers up to additional damages. A manufacturer that is merely ordered to reimburse actual damages to those few consumers who go to court profits from those many consumers who do not go to court.

In Connecticut violation of the state secret warranty law constitutes an unfair trade practice, and in Virginia violation of the secret warranty law constitutes a prohibited practice. The other two states with secret warranty laws, California and Wisconsin, do not make a violation of the law an unfair trade practice. But their laws are new so cases have not yet been decided on whether violation of them constitute an unfair trade practice.

As pointed out in Chapter Seven, secret warranty laws provide powerful emerging legal rights for consumers. For example, Wisconsin allows injured consumers to sue for damages and recover twice the amount of any financial loss, costs and reasonable attorney's fees.

READ IT AND WEEP—
HOW BMW GOT STUCK

In signing the final release or settlement in any litigation make sure all items for which you are seeking reimbursement are included in the agreement. Any omissions are likely to be unfavorable to you, although there are isolated cases when the manufacturer loses out. In *BMW of North America* v. *Krathen*, 471 So.2d 585 (Fl. App. 1985) the Krathens sued for breach of express and implied warranties on their $26,500 automobile which had a front end shimmy that could not be corrected. BMW mailed them an offer to settle the case, that stated that the Krathens could "take judgment against them in the amount of Twenty Thousand Five Hundred ($20,500), plus reasonable attorneys fees and costs heretofore accrued." The Krathens quickly mailed in their acceptance of the offer "as written." BMW filed it with the court, which entered judgment against BMW pursuant to the settlement. BMW later filed a motion to vacate the judgment (to reverse or annul the judgment), however, when it realized that the return of the car was not a condition of the agreement. The court ruled that BMW's failure to include this condition was due to its own inexcusable lack of care in drafting the settlement. BMW's motion was denied, and the Krathen's have both the car and a check for over $20,000.

CLASS ACTIONS

In some situations a class action suit may be the best approach to solving a consumer complaint. A class action is nothing more than a group of individuals sharing a common injury from a product or practice bringing a lawsuit against a manufacturer. For example, a class action may be filed on behalf of all purchasers of the manufacturer's product who suffered in the same way because of a defect in the product. By spreading out the costs of hiring an attorney, a class action reduces each individual's legal fees.

Without a class action, the manufacturer is faced with a few individual claims in small amounts from the few persons persistent enough to see a lawyer and bring an action. With a class action, the manufacturer is faced instead with one gigantic claim representing the total amount lost by each and every victim, even if only a few of those victims are mounting the class action. The class action is potentially one of the most far-reaching devices, legal or nonlegal, available to consumers to redress wrongs.

When consumers win a class action, the defendant may pay the total verdict (often a large amount) into court; individual members of the class then file their own claims for their share of the amount paid into court by the defendant. Class actions are becoming a rallying point of the consumer movement. New York City, for instance, passed a law enabling the city to file class actions for defrauded groups of consumers; its potential effect is indicated by the ferocity with which it is opposed by business interests.

The Magnuson-Moss Warranty Act provides for a class action in federal court where 100 or more named plaintiffs have claims totaling at least $50,000 (exclusive of interests and costs). The Act also makes a provision for the losing manufacturer to pay attorney fees.

The class action provision makes it paramount for consumers with similar defects to band together in order to get the 100 named plaintiffs. Consumers should report their car's defects to the U. S. Department of Transportation (see Chapter Three and Appendix E) and the Center for Auto Safety so that defects common to over 100 consumers can be discovered.

TOYOTA PLAYED AND
PAID—$100 MILLION

When CAS discovered that Toyota was repairing the brake pulsation experienced in 1983–86 Camrys for only those consumers who complained persistently—1000 of whom had complained to CAS alone—it helped the Center for Law in the Public Interest file a class action against the manufacturer. The brake pulsation defect threatened drivers with a loss of control and caused excessive deterioration of the car's tires and lower control arms. A whistle-blower exposed the Toyota secret warranty that authorized free repairs without notifying owners of this defect. Thousands of Camry owners were paying $700-$1,400 for brake pulsation repairs; many of them paid for further damage the defect caused their vehicles. The suit charged Toyota with breach of express and implied warranties, false and misleading advertising, fraud, deceit, breach of obligation of good faith and fair dealing, and unlawful competition.

The precedent-setting suit against Toyota cost the company $100 million. Under the terms of the settlement, Toyota had to notify all 400,000 past and present owners and leasees covered by the suit; they reimbursed out-of-pocket repair and incidental expenses, such as towing and taxis, to consumers who had already fixed their Camrys; repaired any cars in which the defect had not been corrected; arbitrated any disputes through the American Arbitration Association; paid $850,000 into a Consumer Support and Education Fund; and paid $250,000 in attorneys' fees.

CHAPTER 7

STATE SECRET WARRANTY LAWS

Mary Lou Burgess had a lot of problems with her 1985 Buick Park Avenue. The automatic overdrive transmission failed within the first three years. The power steering went out. Information from the Center for Auto Safety showed that her transmission was covered by dozens of Technical Serivce Bulletins and the power steering had a 5 year/50,000 mile secret warranty. Ms. Burgess' situation demonstrates why all states should have secret warranty laws. In a letter to CAS, Mrs. Burgess writes:

> The secret warranty information provided by CAS has helped me recover $5100 in expenses related to serious GM transmission and power steering defects. Hopefully, laws will soon become enacted that will make it illegal for car manufacturers to hide their defects behind 'secret warranties' and save others from going through the ordeal I endured for nearly five years.

If Mrs. Burgess' hopes for secret warranty laws come true, it is likely that states, rather than the federal government, will lead the way. In 1982, Connecticut and California became the first two states to pass lemon laws requiring car companies to replace lemons if they could not be fixed after a reasonable number of repair attempts or days out of service. By 1993, all 50 states had passed lemon laws, while the U.S. Congress looked on, doing nothing.

In 1990, Connecticut was first again in implementing a secret warranty disclosure law. It was followed in 1991 by Virginia, in 1992 by Wisconsin, and in 1994 by California. CAS is working to make the 1990s the decade of secret warranty laws, just as the 1980s saw the passage of 48 states' lemon laws (with the last 2 passed in the '90s).

FAILURE OF THE FEDERAL GOVERNMENT TO EXPOSE SECRET WARRANTIES

There are two situations in which federal law governs defects: If a defect is safety related, federal law specifically requires manufacturers to notify the National Highway Traffic Safety Administration *and owners* of the defect, to recall the cars, and to repair them at no expense. If there are defects involving components intended to keep vehicle emissions within federal requirements, a manufacturer must notify the Environmental Protection Agency and owners, must recall the cars, and must repair them at no expense to the customers. Thus a "secret warranty" for safety related or emissions problems would clearly be unlawful.

Federal law does not require disclosure of secret warranties for other defects. Thus it is up to the Federal Trade Commission (FTC) to use its general consumer protection authority against unfair trade practices to take action on secret warranties. If the FTC, at its discretion, decides not to prosecute, the auto companies do not have to notify consumers of secret warranties on defects that are economic—that is, not safety or environmentally related. Thus manufacturers wait to see what FTC enforcement action will be brought before disclosing secret warranties. And if, as has been the case in the 1980s, the FTC does not prosecute secret warranties, manufacturers can continue the practice and consumers will pay the price.

FTC'S ASSAULT ON
SECRET WARRANTIES IN THE 1970s

Prompted by CAS and thousands of consumer complaints, the Federal Trade Commission (FTC) launched a full scale assault on secret warranties in the 1970s. Charged with the responsibility to fight unfair and deceptive trade practices, the FTC maintained that the failure to disclose widespread manufacturing flaws in a particular model constituted a deceptive trade practice under Section 5 of the Federal Trade Commission Act, particularly where a manufacturer had advertised that its products were reliable and durable.

Some of the early secret warranties were some of the worst. Up until 1973, GM used sperm whale oil as a lubricating fluid in its Type 350 automatic transmissions. When the international ban on whaling took effect, GM changed to a synthetic lubricant which turned out to be incompatible with a solder used in the transmission cooler. Coolant and transmission fluid mixed causing transmission failure which GM paid for under a secret warranty.

Mazda introduced a revolutionary new rotary engine in 1970 before it had perfected the seals at the edges of each rotor. As a result, the engines failed due to inadequate lubrication. Mazda established a secret warranty to cover the cost of replacing engines but specifically ordered its dealers not to tell consumers, with the warning that the secret warranty might be withdrawn at any time.

Chrysler named its infamous "purple people eaters" after a popular song of the day: "one-horned, three-toed, flying purple people eater, sure looks strange to me." They were bright purple and dayglow orange Dodge Daytona's with soaring rear air foils that looked like monsters from outer space that unfortunately sported hugh splotches of peeling paint. For owners who complained loudly, Chrysler repainted the eye sores. Those that did not complain bore the cost of repainting themselves. (Some nonowners felt that the purple people eaters should have been sent to another planet rather than repainted.)

For sheer expense in the early 1970s, Ford held the record with its J-67 rust program. Ford's mid- and full-size cars rusted badly due to inadequate corrosion resistance. Ford adopted an ultra-secret warranty through its zone offices. If a car rusted within 12,000 miles, Ford paid 100% of the repair cost; within 24,000 miles, 75%; within 36,000 miles, 50%; and within 50,000 miles, 25%. Ford kept a heavy lid on this secret warranty because repair costs ran into the thousands of dollars for each vehicle.

Spurred by revelations of costly secret warranties and by petitions from CAS, the FTC began investigating secret warranties in 1974. The FTC considered establishing a rule to abolish secret warranties but rejected the idea because of the number of years it would have taken to issue. The oil industry had already tied up a FTC rule on gasoline quality for twelve years. The FTC feared that the powerful auto industry would tie up secret warranty rulemaking even longer.

The FTC decided the best way to protect consumers from secret warranty abuses was to file enforcement actions against individual auto makers on specific secret warranties and obtain settlements or adjudicatory decisions requiring the auto makers to disclose future secret warranties. Thus the FTC commenced a series of administrative lawsuits against auto makers in which it sought to establish secret warranty disclosure by adjudicatory proceedings rather than rulemaking. In each case against an auto maker for failure to disclose such problems, the FTC sought to require manufacturers to pay for the repairs incurred by all owners.

The FTC assigned lead responsibility in its assault on secret warranties and known defects in motor vehicles to its Cleveland Regional Offices staffed by many attorneys including Paul Peterson (director), Paul Turley (assistant director), Paul Eyre, Larry

Green, Steve Benowitz, and Mel Wolowitz. This small enforcement office soon became the scourge of the auto industry and the champion of the consumer by forcing the auto makers to pay for their defects. The effectiveness of the FTC's Cleveland Regional Office arguably was shown later when the Reagan Administration attempted to abolish it.

The landmark case in the FTC's assault on secret warranties came in 1978 when the Commission sued Ford Motor Company for failing to disclose engine damage and accompanying secret warranties for their repair. Extensive FTC discovery proved the existence of cracked blocks, piston scuffing and camshaft/lifter wear in many of Ford's engines, Ford's knowledge of the defects, and discriminatory secret warranties covering engine repair for consumers who complained loudly. Rather than go to court to face the FTC, armed with all the evidence gathered by its Cleveland Regional Office, Ford settled.

In a landmark consent order that would become the model for future secret warranty decrees with other auto companies, Ford agreed to notify individual owners by first class mail and pay for engine repairs covered by its secret warranty. If the owner had already paid for the repair, Ford reimbursed the consumer. If the repair had not yet been done, Ford agreed to have its dealers do the repair for free. Ford agreed to notify owners of new secret warranties that could cost $25 or more, to provide technical service bulletins, and to set up a toll-free number to provide information on secret warranties (renamed policy adjustments since they were no longer secret). The decree covered powertrain components only and expired after eight years, but the FTC planned to address the problem of non-powertrain components when a good case arose and to seek another decree if Ford continued to offer secret warranties.

Soon after settling the Ford case, the FTC launched an investigation of known defects and secret warranties in GM engines and transmissions, VW engines, Honda and Chrysler rusting fenders, and Mitsubishi engines. But with the change from the pro-consumer Carter Administration to the anti-consumer Reagan Administration in 1981, the FTC sounded a retreat just as its forces seemed poised for victory in the assault on secret warranties.

FTC TAKES A DIVE IN THE 1980s

In 1981 after the change of Administrations, the FTC took a dive in its fight to expose secret warranties. No case better illustrates this than the faulty balance chains on 4-cylinder engines made by Mitsubishi and installed in 1976–77 Colts and Arrows sold through Chrysler Corporation. Failure of the balance chains caused extensive engine damage for which, under a secret warranty, Chrysler paid owners who complained loudly. The Cleveland Office of the FTC investigated the case and got Chrysler to agree to notifying owners about the defect and to reimburse them for repairs. Mitsubishi agreed to pay $5 million in costs to Chrysler but only if the FTC approved the proposed consent agreement. It was an incredible blow to consumers when the Commissioners voted to save Mitsubishi $5 million and rejected the proposed settlement.

The Mitsubishi case signaled the demise of the FTC's efforts to protect consumers from secret warranties. Other cases prepared or filed by the Commission through 1981 were dropped or watered down in the 1980s. Based on a three to two Commission vote, the case against GM on diesel engines, Type 200 automatic transmissions and 305 CID engine camshaft wear was settled with GM agreeing only to submit claims to the Better Business Bureau (BBB) rather than to pay consumers directly as was done in the Ford engine case. In going through BBB arbitration, consumers had to prove their vehicles had defective engines and that GM should pay for repairs. The process was so cumbersome and difficult that many consumers gave up or had valid claims denied.

FTC Chairman Mike Pertschuk disagreed with the ruling that set a precedent of using arbitration rather than automatic reimbursement. He said that sending consumers into arbitration against GM was like sending a team of Chinese students in against the Dallas Cowboys football team. Although GM agreed to set up an 800 number to handle service bulletin requests, GM did not include publication and notification to all consumers of secret warranties.

The Volkswagen engine case followed on the heels of the GM engine defect. In this case, faulty valve stem seals caused excess oil consumption and engine damage. Once again, instead of requiring Volkswagen to reimburse all consumers for engine repairs, the Commission sent consumers through burdensome and unpredictable BBB arbitration.

In 1986, the Commission slammed the door on consumer disclosure of secret warranties when the Ford consent agreement expired. CAS petitioned the FTC to extend the agreement because it had been so effective in forcing Ford to notify owners of nearly one hundred policy adjustments which otherwise would have been secret warranties. But the Commission refused.

The FTC continued to have the statutory authority to take action against unfair or deceptive trade practices. However, the FTC now held that its ability to challenge secret warranties depended on, among other things, whether the benefits to consumers of disclosing necessary repairs outweighed the costs of disclosure.

Even if a strict cost benefit analysis were appropriate, the analysis used by the FTC measured just the manufacturer's cost against the consumer's benefit. A proper cost benefit analysis should have measured all costs against all the benefits. In a May 24, 1989 letter to CAS, former FTC Bureau of Consumer Protection Chief William MacLeod stated:

> If the Commission were to require the disclosure of all adjustment programs, some consumers could benefit. Consumers who might otherwise have paid for a repair could learn about and take advantage of the help offered by the automakers in one of these programs. Requiring such disclosures, of course, would also raise the cost of each adjustment program, as reimbursements go to more beneficiaries. We would expect manufacturers to offer fewer programs unless consumers are willing to pay the increased costs. Consumers ultimately would pay, of course, either through service contracts (which they already buy), or through higher sticker prices.

The Bureau of Consumer Protection ignored economic reality when it decided to protect the auto companies at the expense of consumers. Compelling disclosure of adjustment programs in fact reduces total costs to society. When secret warranties are disclosed, total repair costs decrease because repairs are done soon after defects are found thereby eliminating additional damage of a long-ignored problem. Two examples to prove this point involve timing belts and head gaskets. If either is replaced before it fails, the cost of repair is often less than $200. But if either fails (which happens when the consumer has not been notified that there is a problem) the failure will result in major engine damage costing several thousand dollars. Another cost that can be reduced by disclosing secret warranties is the cost of misdiagnosed repairs. When a particular defect is concealed by a secret warranty, a consumer often repairs the wrong thing—such as replacing the power steering pump instead of the rack and pinion assembly which was true in the GM power steering case.

If the consumer has to continue to pay for the manufacturer's mistakes, where is the manufacturer's incentive to build into its cars durability and quality? The irony of the current situation is that if the manufacturer were to eliminate the problem before releasing a new car, the costs would be far cheaper than the costs of repairing defects. In today's more competitive auto market, it is becoming tougher for the manufacturer with defective cars to pass on all the costs of such repairs to its customer. But there are still an estimated 500 secret warranties currently in place.

While reducing the total costs to society, disclosure would not significantly reduce the total benefits to consumers of adjustment programs. Real world experience shows that required disclosure of post-warranty adjustment programs do not lead to curtailment of the programs. When Ford Motor Company settled the FTC's "piston scuffing" lawsuit, it agreed as part of the settlement to continue to issue publicly all post-warranty programs involving powertrain components in all of its automobiles. During the period of the consent judgment, Ford gained market share which should be attributable in part to increased customer satisfaction.

As the 1990s unfold with a new Administration in office, the FTC may once again assume its role as a protector of the public and challenge auto manufacturers' secret warranties. But the states shouldn't wait for the FTC to renew its fight against secret warranties. Too many consumers are bearing the costs of defects in their vehicles in cases that will never appear before the FTC. The states should enact their own laws requiring disclosure of secret warranties.

SECRET WARRANTY RELIEF IN CALIFORNIA, CONNECTICUT, VIRGINIA, AND WISCONSIN

Relief from secret warranty abuses is just a law away. Because the federal government failed the nation's auto owners by doing nothing to stop the wildfire growth of secret warranties in the 1980s, some states are beginning to enact secret warranty disclosure laws. The state secret warranty laws in California, Connecti-

cut, Virginia, and Wisconsin have common themes and requirements: individual notification to owners, state enforcement, and
reimbursement for relevant repairs already made.

Unfortunately, California's secret warranty law is weaker
than the other three laws since it does not give consumers the right
to sue automakers that violate the secret warranty law and it does
not require manufacturers to make service bulletins available to
consumers. Even so, California consumers are still much better
protected from secret warranties than are the consumers in the
other 46 states without secret warranty laws.

Like the lemon laws, the first secret warranty laws are not
perfect; states will need to go back and pass secret warranty law
II's just as they enacted lemon law II's to plug loopholes used by
the automakers. California needs to be the first to enact secret
warranty law II since its secret warranty law has such big loopholes. All four states need to require automakers to set up toll-free
numbers through which consumers can order copies of Technical
Service Bulletins and notices of policy adjustments or secret warranties.

Notice To Consumers
The four secret warranty laws already enacted are very similar to
one another. All require the manufacturer to notify consumers of
the adoption of a warranty adjustment program by first-class mail
within ninety days of its existence. However it is not clear if the
Virginia law requires manufacturers to notify lessees. The California, Virginia, and Wisconsin secret warranty laws require a manufacturer to give written notification to its dealers of an adjustment
program within thirty days of the program's adoption by the
manufacturer.

All four laws require a dealer to tell a consumer if a repair the
consumer is seeking is covered by an adjustment program as long
as the dealer has been notified as such by the manufacturer (under

the Virginia and Wisconsin laws), or "if the dealer has received a service bulletin concerning such adjustment program or otherwise has knowledge of it" (under the Connecticut law), or "if the dealer has received a service bulletin concerning the adjustment program" (under the California law).

The Connecticut, Virginia, and Wisconsin laws require some type of notification of an individual's rights under the secret warranty law.

Reimbursement for Past Repairs

All four laws require an auto manufacturer establishing an adjustment policy to reimburse eligible consumers who have already paid to have their cars repaired. Consumers must make a written claim for reimbursement within two years of payment for the repair. The manufacturer has to notify the consumer of its decision within twenty-one business days of receiving the consumer's claim for reimbursement. In Virginia, the manufacturer's notification must be in writing. In all four states, if the manufacturer denies the consumer's claim for reimbursement, it must state the specific reasons for the denial in writing.

Availability of Service Bulletins

The Connecticut, Virginia, and Wisconsin secret warranty laws either directly or indirectly require the manufacturer to make available to consumers applicable service bulletins upon request. The Wisconsin statute requires the manufacturer to "upon request, furnish the consumer with any document issued by the manufacturer relating to any adjustment program." The Virginia statute requires the manufacturer to "upon request, furnish the consumer with any document issued by a manufacturer pertaining to any adjustment program or to any condition that may substantially affect vehicle durability, reliability or performance."

The statutory language in all three states is broad enough so that it should cover notices to regional offices which manufacturers have used to hide secret warranties in the past, such as the Ford F-series paint problem. The broad language clearly covers service bulletins since they are always written to address problems in vehicle performance. Unfortunately, all three of these secret warranty laws lack the requirement that the manufacturer establish a toll-free telephone number that consumers can call to ask questions and request service bulletins or other pertinent information.

Ironically, the California law requires dealers to post a notice for purchasers which says, among other things, that they "may obtain" copies of service bulletins, for a fee, from either the manufacturer or NHTSA. The law requires the notice to purchasers to also say in parentheses after the word "manufacturer": "Ask your dealer for the toll-free number." Unfortunately, the California law does not require the automakers to set up a toll-free hotline or to make their service bulletins available to consumers. Since the vast majority of manufacturers do not have toll-free hotlines to get service bulletins, this type of provision is meaningless.

Consumer Rights of Actions

Recognizing that there must be remedies as well as rights, the Connecticut, Virginia and Wisconsin laws provide that consumers can sue the manufacturer for damages if it violates the secret warranty law. In Connecticut, consumers who win in court are entitled to recover actual damages. The court has discretion to award punitive damages and/or equitable relief. In Virginia, victorious consumers are entitled to recover actual damages but not less than $100. The consumer may also be awarded attorney fees and court costs. The court may also make additional orders. In Wisconsin, courts are required by statute to award consumers who prevail in court double their monetary losses plus costs and reasonable attorney fees. The court has discretion to award consumers any appropriate equitable relief necessary, such as ordering the manufacturer to repair the vehicle.

As detailed in Chapter Six, violation of the secret warranty disclosure law may violate the state unfair and deceptive trade practices law.

Case-by-Case Adjustments

None of the state secret warranty laws requires that a manufacturer give notice of adjustments made on a case-by-case basis. No one would argue that an auto company that makes an occasional goodwill adjustment on a case-by-case establishes a secret warranty. On the other hand, a manufacturer such as Honda or Toyota which routinely refers consumers with known defects to the regional office for goodwill assistance clearly has a secret warranty and should come under any secret warranty disclosure law.

In implementing its law, Wisconsin clearly recognizes this problem and appears to be poised to go after secret warranties disguised as goodwill adjustments. In a public memorandum on the Wisconsin secret warranty law, the Wisconsin Department of Transportation writes, "Because the law doesn't say how many case-by-case 'individual adjustments' for the same problem or condition make up a 'secret warranty' or what conditions 'substantially affect' vehicle durability, reliability or performance, the courts will ultimately decide those issues." (See Appendix I for a copy of the Wisconsin memo on implementation of its secret warranty law.)

States Without Secret Warranty Laws Should Enact Them

There are several reasons why the other 46 states need to enact secret warranty laws. First, while it is possible that the Federal Trade Commission will resume its consumer protection mission and seek to prosecute the auto companies for using secret warranties, such cases will take years for results and will depend upon the vagaries of administrative policy.

Second, it is unfair for the auto makers to grant free repairs to some consumers, but not to others with identical problems. Only customers who complain persistently, or are particularly valued by a dealer, get the benefits of a secret warranty program. This runs contrary to the equitable notion that persons similarly situated are entitled to similar treatment.

Third, it is unfair, wasteful and costly when a manufacturer knows of defects which, if not repaired, will cause expensive problems in the future, but fails to advise consumers, who then have no opportunity to prevent the likely future damage. A prime example of this problem is the widespread failure of the engine oil pressure sending unit in certain Toyotas covered under a secret warranty program. This $37 unit often failed, making it impossible for Toyota owners to know when their engines needed oil. As a result, many owners experienced catastrophic engine failure and astronomical bills for a replacement engine that could have been avoided if Toyota had notified them of the secret warranty and hidden defect.

There are many other examples of cases where manufacturers failed to widely disclose the need for inexpensive repairs for such items as oil filters, warning lights, and other components, even though the auto makers knew that expensive repairs would result from their failure to do so.

Fourth, because many consumers take their cars to independent shops after expiration of the written warranty, especially for expensive repair work, they have no opportunity to learn about or benefit from secret warranty programs. This harms both consumers who must pay for the repair and manufacturers, whose customers are unhappy about the repair costs. Moreover, because the defects are often difficult to diagnose without repair instructions that manufacturers provide only to their dealers, consumers often pay for unnecessary repairs due to mistaken diagnoses or for ineffective repair attempts.

Fifth, properly drafted secret warranty laws in the states without them would clarify the duties of both manufacturers and dealers. Such legislation should require manufacturers to provide complete disclosure of post-warranty adjustment programs, notice to customers by first class mail, establishment of a toll-free telephone system to provide information about such programs, free indexes to all service bulletins, and free bulletins on secret warranties and reduced cost for all other bulletins. It should also require dealers to both notify customers of repairs covered under such programs and to perform the work at no charge or under the reduced-cost terms of the program. The legislation should also provide a private right of action for consumers with mandatory attorney fees, costs and treble damages for violation of the secret warranty law. (See Appendix K for a model law.)

Sixth, automakers operate within a free market system that rewards quality and efficiency. A government requirement that defects be disclosed is fully consistent with a free market system. In the long run, automakers who fail to manufacture reliable, durable vehicles at low cost will lose business.

Viewed in the long-term perspective, requiring disclosure of post-warranty adjustment programs will further the efficiency of the marketplace. Properly informed, consumers will choose vehicles from companies that make the best products and which stand behind their products in the event that a widespread problem develops.

Finally, secret warranty laws help to force a manufacturer to pay for latent, widespread product defects. They help to give the manufacturer the proper incentive to pursue the least cost approach, which is to build higher quality cars with fewer defects. If manufacturers are compelled to notify consumers of prevalent, latent defects that are covered by adjustment programs, they will only be able to pass some of the costs of latent, widespread defects onto consumers in the form of higher priced cars. The automobile industry is fiercely competitive. If a manufacturer tried to pass on too many costs to consumers, it would lose market share. And market share is crucial to obtaining or maintaining economies of scale that are necessary to be a low cost producer.

If disclosure of adjustment programs were compelled, the competitiveness of the auto market would assure that stockholders, not consumers, bear most of the costs of latent, widespread defects. Wealth would be neither wasted nor squandered, merely shifted. Ultimately the true question is who should bear the economic costs of poor product quality: stockholders or consumers?

CHAPTER 8

ARBITRATION

A fter you have exhausted all remedies within the manufacturer's complaint handling mechanism, you may want to submit
your claim to arbitration. The Center for Auto Safety generally
advises use of small claims court instead of arbitration for secret
warranty cases; small claims courts almost invariably rule for the
consumer when presented with a documented secret warranty. But
arbitration offers a relatively quick and inexpensive way to gain
recompense in a secret warranty case. If it doesn't work, consumers can still pursue their claim in small claims court since auto
company-run arbitration is not binding.

Many consumers receive full reimbursement in arbitration
for repairs made on a defect covered by a secret warranty. For
example, Howard Ekerling of Sherman Oaks, California wrote the
Center for Auto Safety:

> I want to thank you for your work on the 'blushing
> paint' secret warranty on 1985 black Cadillac automo-
> biles. GM denied my requests for reimbursement, so I
> demanded arbitration. The arbitrator awarded in my favor,
> and GM paid in full for the entire cost of the paint job.

Arbitration is an informal proceeding, in which you and the
manufacturer's representative present your case before an arbitra-

tor or a panel of arbitrators. Presentations are made either in writing, or there is an oral hearing and you must appear in person. In all instances, the arbitrators are supposed to be independent of the manufacturer.

Some manufacturer-run arbitration panels, such as Chrysler's, allow written submissions only, making the need to document and support your case even more crucial; you are not given an opportunity to explain any discrepancies between your submission and the manufacturer's.

Robert and Joan Farmer of San Diego, California experienced severe surging problems with their new Chrysler. The car was in the shop for more than 30 days in its first six months of ownership, so they decided to seek a buyback under California's lemon law. First, they took their case to the Chrysler Customer Satisfaction Board, which told them they did not have to be present because the dealer involved was not going to appear. But they insisted on appearing, as was their right under the lemon law. At the hearing, the Board reported that a Chrysler representative had claimed that the Farmers had not picked up their car when it was ready for repair, a fact crucial to their case because of the 30 day trigger under the lemon law. This allegation was untrue; since the Farmers appeared at the hearing, they were able to dispute it. They reported this misinterpretation to the FTC, as should you if there is any procedural unfairness or irregularity in your arbitration. You should also report such infractions to your state Attorney General, state and federal legislators, and any consumer group in your jurisdiction that could intercede on your behalf.

Most arbitration proceedings routinely involve an oral hearing, where you can question—and be questioned about—the facts of your case. Usually no one else is present except for witnesses brought by either side and an arbitrator (or panel of arbitrators). No formal rules of evidence or procedure are followed; instead, the arbitrator generally accepts all of the documentation and testimony of each side (within reason) and considers it. The arbitrator then makes his or her decision shortly after the hearing.

Preparation for arbitration is similar to the preparation for small claims court: bring good documentation and organize your facts about the defects and repairs. If you know your case well, have organized your evidence so that it can be clearly and logically presented, and have a good understanding of what you must prove to gain reimbursement, you should have an excellent chance of winning.

Unfortunately, the arbitration programs are not always run in compliance with their own rules. Gary M. Long of Concord, NC found this out when he went to BBB arbitration to get GM to repair the transmission that it had already replaced once on his 1986 Buick LeSabre. He wrote CAS:

> I was surprised that BBB did not follow their own procedures in setting up the hearing in that I was not given written notification of the hearing nor allowed a choice of hearing officers. Hearing notifications were made by phone. On the day of the hearing, I presented evidence of the replacement of the transmission, and supporting data on the problems Buick had experience[d] with both the transmission and general quality problems with that model year. Unfortunately the hearing officer was not convinced that the problem was Buick's, based solely on the mileage of the car, and he denied any compensation.
>
> Not satisfied with the outcome, I filed suit in small claims court for the transmission repair and for costs incurred in replacing the camshaft endplate with a redesigned model.
>
> Dedicated to convincing the judge of the problems I had had, I went to court with a 2 inch stack of service bulletins on the transmission, paid invoices, magazine

articles on overall Buick quality, and a prepared statement on my problems with the car. After hearing my evidence the judge allowed the GM local representative to present his case, which began with the fact that I had lost my case in BBB arbitration. Beyond that there was basically no defense that he could offer to offset the weight of evidence that I had presented, (about 8 pounds of paper). . . .

The outcome was good for me because the judge awarded me $1,337.00 for the transmission repair and the camshaft plate.

Even after the court decision Buick legal people tried to get me to sign a release that I would not seek any further compensation on this vehicle. I responded that I would have the local court officers collect the money since it was court ordered and that I refused to sign anything. I received the check in about 5 days.

Hope this helps the next consumer who gets stuck by the "Big Guys."

PREPARATION FOR ARBITRATION: KNOW THE RULES

Once you decide to arbitrate, contact the organization running the arbitration, whether it is the Better Business Bureau, a manufacturer's appeals board, a state-run board, or the American Arbitration Association, to find out what the rules are. Explain exactly what you are seeking and ask for a complaint form to initiate the process. Request a copy of any printed information that explains the program. Familiarize yourself with all steps in the process so you do not miss any deadlines or requests for information. Ask questions about anything you do not fully understand or agree with; remember, the manufacturer has had a lot more experience than you have with this process, and will send an experienced representative to the hearing. Give yourself the best chance possible to prevail by becoming fully informed of the process.

It is particularly important to know if your car is eligible for arbitration pursuant to an FTC consent order. For example, as a settlement of its complaint against GM for its lemon diesels and certain specified components, the FTC ordered the company to arbitrate claims involving the powertrain through the Better Business Bureau, regardless of the age or mileage of the vehicle, through 1991. In spite of this clear directive, some local BBB offices erroneously rejected claims to arbitrate, and many arbitrators denied relief because the car was "too old" to qualify for reimbursement or replacement.

When Paul and Ethel Lubarsky contacted the BBB in Farmingdale, New York, the office told them they were ineligible for arbitration because the car was five years old and had over 50,000 miles on it. But the Lubarskys had read several articles on the consent order, had secured letters from both the FTC and GM stating they met the arbitration requirements, and contacted the Council of Better Business Bureaus in Arlington, Virginia with their complaint. They were finally granted a hearing, more than a year after their original application.

FIND OUT IF THE PROGRAM IS BINDING

Before you begin arbitration, find out if the arbitration decision will be binding on you. If so, you cannot seek future relief and you should consider other arbitration programs you can use, or foregoing this step to go right to court. A lawsuit is more time consuming and costly, but it presents you the opportunity to seek more damages (such as the cost of a rental car) than in arbitration, and the right to appeal if you don't agree with the findings.

BE SPECIFIC ABOUT WHAT
YOU WANT AS A REMEDY

To initiate the process, you have to indicate to the arbitration program exactly what relief you are seeking. For example, the

BBB will send you a form called "Agreement to Arbitrate," which states exactly what is subject to arbitration. Read this form carefully. You cannot be awarded anything other than that which is stated in this agreement, so make sure everything you seek is clearly written out. It is very important to include a complete list of all expenses or repairs for which you seek reimbursement in the agreement. The arbitrator is bound by the terms of this agreement and it determines what he or she is authorized to award you.

La Vonne Slama of Gresham, Oregon found out about this limit the hard way when she was awarded a $10,700 buyback of her 1984 Oldsmobile Cutlass, but denied several thousand dollars in additional expenses not listed on the agreement to arbitrate. She complained to CAS that:

> The Oregon BBB office is one of the most poorly informed programs that I have ever seen. They do not tell you that if you do not put all your costs in your complaint that you can't add to them. Thus we did get a buyback but no reimbursement for down payment nor out-of-pocket expenses.

In general, you may arbitrate any vehicle problem for up to the purchase price of the car *plus* repair bills. You don't have to ask for money; you may ask for a needed repair which the manufacturer and/or the dealer has not performed. Normally arbitration will not cover such expenses as substitute transportation, lodging, lost wages or other incidental or consequential damages. Nevertheless, you should ask for compensation for these damages; it is up to the program to explain if they are not eligible, and the arbitrator may be influenced by these other damages in deciding the award for covered damages. In at least eight states—Connecticut, District of Columbia, Kansas, Maine, Maryland, Massachusetts, Mississippi Vermont and West Virginia—you will usually be able to recover incidental and consequential damages under state law, but the manufacturer may not agree to submit these issues to arbitration. If arbitration does not cover these expenses, you may later file in small claims court to get them.

MEDIATION BEFORE ARBITRATION

After you've initiated the arbitration process, some programs will attempt to mediate your case by forwarding your complaint to the manufacturer, which may attempt to work out a settlement with you. The majority of complaints end at this point. It is not known whether consumers are satisfied with the settlement offer or simply accept out of frustration. Do not feel pressured to settle if you are not satisfied with what the company offers. As long as you meet the eligibility requirements, you have the right to present your case to an arbitrator.

William Crawford of Phoenix, Arizona was one consumer who benefited greatly by not ending his case during mediation. The BBB originally mediated a settlement of $325 with GM for his 1983 Oldsmobile Cutlass, and advised him to accept it, since depreciation losses were not subject to arbitration. He decided *not* to accept the settlement and took his case to arbitration where he was awarded $8,256 for a buyback of the car, which had 41,123 miles on it at the time of the hearing.

PREPARE YOUR CASE THOROUGHLY

If the mediation process does not work to your satisfaction, then you can go on to arbitration. The key to success in arbitration is documentation and organization. To clarify the case for your own sake and for your oral presentation and to make it easy for the arbitrator to award you a reimbursement, have a summary of all repairs and breakdowns relating to the defect covered by the secret warranty listed in chronological order, with the relevant date and mileage indicated next to each entry. Have copies of corresponding receipts, correspondence, and repair orders labeled and ready to present to both the arbitrator and the manufacturer's representative.

It is essential that you have evidence that the defect is covered by a secret warranty. Most important, you should get copies of the service bulletins applicable to the defect from the National Highway Traffic Safety Administration (NHTSA). You also may be able to get service bulletins from the dealer or the manufacturer. (See Chapter Three on how to gather this type of information.) In addition to getting the relevant service bulletins, you should research any newspaper and magazine articles about your secret warranty, and bring copies of any such articles. Obtain a computer printout of complaints NHTSA has received on your particular problem. You should also have either a notarized statement or an affidavit from a mechanic or other automotive expert, if possible, which states what problems your car has. This will help negate the argument made by the manufacturer that the problem is your fault, caused by lack of maintenance or poor driving habits. (Both of these tactics are commonly used by automakers.)

Gather all relevant evidence and make arrangements with potential witnesses well in advance of the arbitration hearing. If the manufacturer or its dealer have evidence or witnesses (such as a dealer's mechanic) that you need to make your case in arbitration, you should write them well before the hearing to request that they send you the evidence promptly or agree that the witnesses you need will be at the hearing. If the evidence or agreement to testify is not provided voluntarily, it may be possible to write the program to request that the arbitrator issue a "subpoena." Even if the arbitrator does not issue a subpoena, give the arbitrator a copy of your request to the manufacturer or dealer and ask the arbitrator to rule in your favor on the facts that would have been revealed by the evidence or witnesses that they refused to provide.

ARBITRATION AT LAST

At this point, you and the manufacturer have not reached a settlement through mediation, so the program with which you have filed your complaint will arrange an arbitration hearing. Recontact them to ensure they do. These hearings should be held within a specified number of days from the date you filed your complaint; refer to the program rules for this information. You may have the choice of a personal hearing, a telephone conference call or submission of your case in writing. A personal hearing is the best way to make your claim. It may be necessary for you to travel a short distance to accommodate the proceeding, but every effort should be made to make the hearing location convenient for you, especially if your car is not operable.

SELECTING AN ARBITRATOR

You may have the option of choosing an arbitrator from a list of potential candidates that will be provided with brief biographical sketches included. Eliminate any from the list with whom you have a conflict—a business or personal relationship—and rank the rest according to your preference. The arbitration program will select a single arbitrator or a panel of three based on the preferences indicated by you and the auto company. Most of the manufacturer-run panels are comprised of representatives from the auto industry and consumers.

Some auto companies' arbitration panels are run by manufacturer representatives only. You will not have a choice of arbitrator in this situation.

INSPECTION OF YOUR CAR

If you want the arbitrator to inspect your car, make your request well before your hearing; the inspection will take up considerable time during the arbitration. You may also request the arbitrator to provide a neutral expert to inspect your vehicle and to submit findings at the hearing. The arbitrator decides whether an inspection or expert will be provided. In some cases, if the vehicle is inoperable, the manufacturer must arrange to tow it to the hearing at its cost. You can always hire your own expert and present his or her findings at the hearing, or have the expert appear at the hearing to present testimony.

MAKING YOUR CASE IN ARBITRATION

The key to success in arbitration is thorough advance preparation. You should collect, organize, and be knowledgable about all the evidence you are bringing to your hearing. The testimony and the evidence you submit will not be restricted to legal rules of evidence, except that neither you nor the manufacturer may contact the arbitrator outside of the hearing unless the other side is present or has given written permission. Insist on receiving copies of any documents that the manufacturer's representative presents to the arbitrator in support of its case. The manufacturer's representative may likewise request copies of your documents. Both you and the manufacturer's representative may question the other's witnesses.

At the hearing, explain to the arbitrator in your own words what happened to your car, what the mileage was at the time, and what the manufacturer and its dealer did or did not do about it. Be as specific as possible about how much it cost to repair the defect covered by the secret warranty and other expenses caused by the defect. Support your explanation with repair bills, mechanic's testimony, any letters written to the dealer or manufacturer, and any other evidence of the problem.

List your money losses or damages caused by the defect covered by the secret warranty. Have a copy of a bill for every expense, if possible. Ask for full reimbursement of these expenses. Even if your arbitration does not cover incidental or consequential damages such as towing charges, lodging or transportation, list them anyway. The arbitrator may decide to increase the award to implicitly cover such damages.

If you win reimbursement for repair of a defect covered by a secret warranty through arbitration and do not recover incidental expenses such as towing, lodging or rental cars, file for these in small claims court. In small claims court you can introduce the arbitration award as evidence of the defect and secret warranty. If the automaker does not settle before your court hearing, be sure to tell the judge you are seeking these incidental damages in small claims court because they did not fall within the jurisdiction of arbitration.

BASE YOUR CASE ON COMMON SENSE, FAIRNESS, AND APPLICABLE LAW

The guiding principle of arbitration is ruling based on what is fair or reasonable. Technically, the arbitration is not governed by law as is a court case, so you should not assume that an arbitrator is familiar with the law applicable to your case. Nevertheless, you should become familiar with the most important aspects of the applicable law and make arguments based on the law. You should suggest to the arbitrator that a just decision should give you at least that which the law entitles you to.

Warranty law is most relevant to your complaint. Your case could involve an implied warranty, an express warranty, and/or a federal or state mandated warranty. If you live in one of the four states that have enacted secret warranty legislation—California, Connecticut, Virginia, and Wisconsin—then make sure you understand what you are entitled to under that law.

Emphasize to the arbitrator that the length of the written warranty does not govern the arbitration, nor does any decision rendered supersede or overrule any terms of the warranty. Rather, as noted above, the basic principles of arbitration are common sense, fairness, and justice. Thus, your task is to convince the arbitrator that it is fair for you to receive the benefit of the secret warranty since other consumers are allowed to benefit from it. Stress that it is deceptive for a manufacturer who learns of a common, material defect to keep that knowledge a secret from its customers. Finally, emphasize that concealing known defects and secret warranties is an unfair trade practice which every state prohibits.

Argue that a secret warranty demonstrates the existence of a manufacturing defect that was in your vehicle on the day it was sold to you and that this is a breach of both the express and implied warranties that come with your car. If the defect covered by the secret warranty caused your car to sustain further damages because the defect went unrepaired (e.g. defective engine oil pressure sending unit causes catastrophic engine failure), argue that the manufacturer should have to bear these costs also.

Normally manufacturers attempt to limit implied warranties to the same length as their written warranties, but in at least six states—District of Columbia, Maine, Maryland, Massachusetts, Vermont, and West Virginia—they are prohibited from limiting implied warranties for consumer goods. In those states it is especially clear that the manufacturer is responsible for hidden defects that pop up after the written warranty. Note that Connecticut, Kansas, and Mississippi do not allow implied warranties on consumer goods to be limited in most cases. (See Chapter Six for more information on warranty rights.)

Many consumers have reported to CAS that their arbitrator erroneously believed that the written warranty was controlling. Emphasize that the written warranty period does not govern the arbitration result. For instance, the Federal Trade Commission issued specific instructions that the terms of the written warranty do not define the scope of a manufacturer's liability and a consumer may recover for failure regardless of mileage. In the case of GM engines, and transmissions and VWoA engines, the Federal

Trade Commission issued specific instructions that the terms of the written warranty do not define the scope of a manufacturer's liability and a consumer may recover for failure regardless of mileage.

RESPONSES TO THE
MANUFACTURER'S DEFENSES

The manufacturer may claim that many breakdowns are due to inadequate maintenance, or even your abuse of the car. In this way, the manufacturer suggests to the arbitrator that you are to blame for your car's problems. While it is the manufacturer's burden to prove that you were at fault, you will present the strongest case by showing you took good care of your car and maintained it properly. Bring service records if you have them, or testimony from your mechanic. Even letters from friends who know your driving habits or how you care for your car can help. Articles or other materials showing your problem is part of a widespread defect in your model are also helpful. If you have driven cars in the past without any problem, state this fact. Even if you do not have thorough records, point out to the arbitrator that the FTC says the lack of thorough records is not controlling. Remember that the manufacturer must prove that your car received improper maintenance. Have your owner's manual handy and don't let the manufacturer charge you with more maintenance obligations than are listed in your manual.

REOPENING THE HEARING
FOR ADDITIONAL INFORMATION

With some programs you may request that the hearing be reopened before the decision is made to consider additional evidence. Write to the arbitration board and they should forward the request to the other party and the arbitrator, who decides whether there is enough additional evidence to reopen the hearing. You can only get a hearing reopened if you can present "new evidence" that was unavailable at the time of the hearing, e.g., if you locate a missing witness.

RECONSIDERATION OF YOUR CASE

If you believe the final decision is impossible to perform by its terms, contains a misstatement of the facts of your case, or contains an error in calculation (such as a mistake in the subtraction of deductions taken), immediately contact the program in writing. If the decision is too unspecific or it is unclear how it is to be executed, you may have grounds for reconsideration. The program should forward your notice to the other parties in the case for review, but it is strictly up to the arbitrator whether the decision will be modified.

If a consumer can show a hearing was tainted by impropriety, contact the national program and ask for a new hearing. Richard Howell of Irvine, California asked the BBB for another hearing after the arbitrator in his first hearing refused to accept evidence presented by Mr. Howell, including published defect data and a tape of Mr. Howell's car showing its hard start condition. The national Council of BBB's in Virginia told the local BBB, "In an effort to provide fairness in our arbitration programs, the Council is requesting your office to rehear the entire case with a new arbitrator." Three months later the second arbitrator awarded Mr. Howell a full purchase price buyback of $17,809 for his Cadillac with 40,000 miles.

AFTER THE FINAL DECISION

Once the decision is final, you have to decide whether to accept or reject it. If you want to accept it, make sure you notify the program of your acceptance within the time specified in its letter to you, or the decision will be considered rejected and the manufacturer can refuse to comply with the decision. If you reject it, you retain your rights to pursue other recourse against the manufacturer, including a lawsuit. If you accept what is offered, it is a legally binding resolution of all issues that were arbitrated. Thus, make sure you can live with what you are accepting. You should receive the full benefit of the manufacturer's secret warranty if it's applicable to your car. If the decision calls for repairs, it should state where the repairs are to be performed and when they are to be completed so you are not stuck for months while the shop "is working on it." The time allowed should be no more than 30 days from your acceptance of the decision. The decision should also state that if you have any problems within a specified "interim period" after the repairs have been completed (generally 30–45 days), you have the right to reconvene the hearing to seek a more satisfactory resolution. If the repaired problem reappears after the interim period has passed, you can file for a new arbitration hearing.

If you reject the decision entirely or were unable to submit for arbitration all of the claims you are entitled to (such as incidental expenses) you can proceed to small claims court. Bruce Knight of St. Paul, Minnesota was awarded $3,200 for the buyback of his 1982 Oldsmobile Cutlass after he submitted records of the car's crankshaft problems, transmission malfunctions, and fuel injector pump defects, which made his car a moving fire hazard. After the arbitrator's award, he then won $1,000 in small claims court for ancillary costs not subject to arbitration, such as insurance, rental car expenses, and towing charges. (Chapter Nine explains how to use the court system to file your claim.)

HOW TO ENFORCE AN
ARBITRATION AWARD

If the manufacturer fails to carry out an arbitration award, first contact the program board. Even if they cannot compel the manufacturer to comply voluntarily with the decision, they are authorized to arrange for an attorney for you to enforce the decision in court, and to charge the manufacturer for your litigation costs. You must first contact the program before bringing suit, however, to see if you qualify for this arrangement. If they can't help, you can bring a suit on your own to enforce the decision. Of course, auto makers nearly always comply with arbitration awards, so most consumers that win in arbitration do not have to worry about enforcing their awards.

CHAPTER 9

SMALL CLAIMS COURTS

An Auto Giant Takes a Fall
by Jim Brewer

An extremely disenchanted customer took the world's largest automobile manufacturer to court and won. It happened in Marin County small claims court where attorneys are forbidden to participate.

Judge Robert A. Smallman ordered the Chevrolet division of General Motors to reimburse a 37-year-old geologist for the cost of replacing the engine in his 1972 Vega. The car broke down last year with just over 25,000 miles on it.

It was a victory for John T. O'Rourke of San Anselmo who said he decided "to fight it out" in small claims court because "it was me against them—no high powered lawyers."

Under court rules, he will only collect $500 of the $678.83 it cost him to repair the engine, but O'Rourke said it was worth it. Five hundred dollars is the maximum claim allowed in small claims court.

"The consumer has been shafted too often," he said. "The people who buy this kind of car just can't afford to put a new engine in."

O'Rourke made his case based upon a three-month old consumer report which urged the Federal Trade Commission to require that auto makers notify car owners of any warranty extensions.

The report, by the Center for Auto Safety in Washington, D.C., said "General Motors and other automobile manufacturers sometimes double the life of a warranty (to two years or 24,000 miles) for selected owners . . . without disclosing such extensions to the public or the affected owner."

It specifically cited "under the table extensions by General Motors on 1971 and '72 Vegas because the cooling systems in these models often break down."

The report did not say who the "selected owners" were, but O'Rourke wasn't one of them.

GM officials said the damage to the car was due to "excessive hard carbon buildup on the pistons" and not "product failure." William Perry, a Chevrolet Motors representative, told Judge Smallman that warranties were not selectively extended to some Vega owners but said his company, in some instances, "made policy adjustments to keep our customers happy."

"The way I see it, policy adustments and warranty extensions are the same thing," Judge Smallman said. And he ordered Chevrolet to pay O'Rourke $500 plus $27 in court costs.

San Francisco Chronicle, April 23, 1974
Copyright Chronicle Publishing Co., 1974

John T. O'Rourke's victory against an auto giant in small claims court has now become so commonplace that newspapers do not write about them anymore. But they should—just to continue to chronicle the victory of the little consumer against the corporate giant. In the area of secret warranties, CAS has received success story after success story as consumers have taken on GM, Ford, Toyota and all the other auto giants and won.

Small claims courts, designed to provide a fast, efficient, and inexpensive way to resolve claims of individuals against merchants or large corporations, are potentially a great resource to consumers. They are one of the best ways for consumers to settle disputes with a dealer, service station, repair shop, garage, or auto manufacturer.

Small claims court is just what it sounds like—a forum for claims not large enough to warrant a full-scale trial, yet worthy of argument before a judge. Virtually every state has small claims courts, each generally having county-wide jurisdiction. Claim limits range from $1,000–10,000, which means that this is not the appropriate court to seek considerable damages and expenses. Since most defects covered by secret warranties cost from a few hundred to a few thousand dollars to repair, small claims courts are ideal forums to haul in a recalcitrant manufacturer that refuses to pay up under a secret warranty.

A major advantage to small claims courts is that they are so simple you don't have to hire a lawyer to represent you; in fact, some courts do not permit lawyers. Even if the automaker brings in high-priced lawyers to fight your claim, as Chrysler did with Toby Cagan (see page 197), do not be intimidated or discouraged. Small claims court is meant to provide an informal, simple method of justice where consumers can easily explain their problem and the remedy they seek. The judge may help present the case by asking appropriate questions. Formal courtroom procedures and the use of legal rules are usually ignored, providing an informal atmosphere in which consumers making claims can more easily talk out their problem before the judge.

Information and other resources are available for the consumer to use in preparing to go to small claims court. A few courts and many consumers groups and agencies publish guides or consumer manuals on using small claims courts, with emphasis on the local procedures involved. (See Appendix H for list of titles and where they can be obtained.) Even though a lawyer is usually not necessary in a small claims court suit, some legal assistance or advice may be helpful. Free legal help may be obtained from law students who are participating in a legal clinic, such as the Law Students in Court Program in Washington, D.C. Call the nearest law school to find out whether there is such a program in your area. Often legal assistance is available from neighborhood legal service organizations or legal aid societies that are set up to help low-income or minority groups. Where legal assistance is necessary some courts will provide indigent consumers with a lawyer at the consumer's request.

PROCEDURES

Filing a Complaint

Small claims courts are located in county or other local court-houses in your state. The plaintiff (person who is suing) usually must file suit in the area or district where the defendant (person being sued) lives, works, or has his or her place of business; for example, where the dealership is located.

The small claims court in your area will be listed in the telephone book under Courts for either your city or county government, or there may be a general information number for Courts. (See Appendix F for a small claims court directory indicating for each state the type of court, availability of appeals, maximum amount of suit, use of lawyers, and where the procedure is informal.)

After finding the court in your area, ask to speak to the clerk of the small claims court. Tell the clerk that you wish to file a complaint. Ask the clerk whether the court can handle your kind of case and whether it has jurisdiction over the party (or parties) you wish to sue. As a general rule, the defendant must live, work, or do business in the court's territory. Since automobile manufacturers do business in all areas of the country, they can be sued in just about every small claims court. Thus, choose the court in an area where the dealership is located when suing the dealer and manufacturer.

The clerk can assist in filling out the necessary form. The basic and perhaps only form you need to fill out is the complaint. Many small claims courts will have a sample, filled out, complaint available. The complaint includes your name and address, the name and address of the person whom you are suing, the amount of your claim and the reason for your suit. (See Appendix G for a sample complaint.)

Be certain the business name of the organization you are suing (which you write on the complaint) is the official *legal* title. John's GM Shop may not be enough; it may be legally registered as John Brown's General Motors Showroom, Inc. Some courts will dismiss the suit unless the company is identified in the complaint exactly as it is registered for legal purposes. Ask the court clerk whether the exact legal name is required, and if so, how to find the correct name. This information can usually be checked with the city or county clerk, or the state secretary of state. See if the dealership or repair shop has an operating license posted on an office wall with the legal name on it.

In secret warranty cases, the auto company is the primary, if not the sole defendant. This makes life simple since auto companies are required to have an agent for service of process in almost every state under a so-called "long arm" statute designed to make out-of-state corporations subject to local lawsuits. According to the office of CT Corporation Systems in Washington, D.C., CT Corporation Systems is an agent to receive service of process for the automakers in all 50 states. Because this sometimes changes, verify that CT is an agent for the particular automaker involved in your state by contacting the state secretary of state or the official keeper of corporate records in your state. The address and phone number for CT Corporation Systems' national headquarters is as follows:

CT Corporation Systems
1633 Broadway
New York, NY 10019
(212) 246-5070

New York Residents Beware

Beware of tricky statues like the one in New York which effectively precludes consumers from recovering under secret warranties in small claims courts. In New York, small claims courts restrict suits to companies having a place of business within the county in which the suit is brought. The car companies cannot be directly sued in small claims court in the New York Counties in which they do not have a place of business.

Car companies can still be brought to justice in these counties in New York but consumers living there have to work a little harder to do so. These consumers could sue in regular civil court and use the long arm statute to serve the auto company's agent. Consumers should not worry about the increased formality of civil court since the auto company is likely to settle if the consumer attaches a copy of the secret warranty document to the complaint. Consumers in New York have even won lemon buybacks in civil court without lawyers so don't be intimidated by bringing a little secret warranty claim in regular civil court because the New York State legislature made it difficult for many New York consumers to bring car companies to justice.

A consumer could also sue both the dealer and the auto company in small claims court in the county in which the dealer is located. Service of process on the auto company can be made on the dealer on the theory that the franchised dealer is also the manufacturer's place of business. Even if the court does not uphold service of the auto company, the consumer can argue that the dealer should pay the secret warranty claim since the manufacturer has authorized the dealer to carry out the secret warranty repair. However, a consumer should not have to jump through such hoops to get justice in a state like New York which claims to be a leader in consumer protection.

Damages—What the Consumer Gets

The very least a consumer should seek in small claims court is the full amount or benefit of the secret warranty. Whatever the terms of the secret warranty, that's the absolute least a consumer should get. If the secret warranty pays the full cost for repairing a defect, then the minimum damages are the cost of repair plus the cost of bringing the lawsuit. If the secret warranty pays for only half the repair, sue for the entire repair cost since a manufacturing defect obviously existed in your vehicle which should be covered by an express or implied warranty. After all, the manufacturer has admitted there's a defect by establishing a secret warranty. Its decision to pay only part of the repair is arbitrary and unilateral and should be overturned by the court.

Consumers should sue for incidental and consequential damages such as towing and failure of other parts caused by the secret warranty defect. For example, assume that a car's engine oil pressure sending unit is covered by a secret warranty such as the one Toyota had for several of its 1983 and 1984 vehicles including the Celica, Corolla, Supra, and Cressida. If the car's engine suffers catastrophic failure because the owner didn't know the engine had lost oil pressure, it's because Toyota failed to notify the consumer of the defect. If the consumer had known of the secret warranty, he or she would have gotten the oil pressure sending unit fixed and would not have had an engine failure. The pressure sending unit is a direct damage which the consumer suffered and can clearly recover. The cost of the replacement engine is a consequential damage to which the consumer is also entitled. Finally, if the owner had to pay a towing charge and alternative transportation, the owner should sue for these as incidental damages.

When you fill out the complaint, be precise. State exactly what part of the car is covered by the secret warranty. If you have a copy of the auto company's bulletin showing a secret warranty, attach that and your repair order for the defect covered by the secret warranty to the complaint. If you can do this, you should be a hands down winner who gets a call from the auto company's lawyer saying they will pay up.

The clerk will give you a summons to be completed with the complaint. A summons is the official notification of the case delivered to the party you are suing, which will be sent to the defendant after you have filed your complaint. Serve the dealer at the dealership. For the auto company, serve the registered agent. For most major auto companies this is CT Corporation. Most states require that you serve the registered agent by certified mail.

After you fill out the forms, you will pay a small filing fee which usually will be returned if you win since the losing party pays it. The clerk will then give you a copy of the forms and usually a "docket number" (identifying the case) and a date for the hearing of your case. The hearing date is usually scheduled for 2–8 weeks from the date of filing. Some courts notify plaintiffs by mail telling them whether the defendant was served with the summons. If the defendant cannot be located you are responsible for finding the address where they can be served.

Preparing Your Case
Try to attend a session of the court to learn the procedure so you will know what to expect and how to prepare for your own hearing.

At least come to court early on the hearing date and observe the cases that come up before yours, in order to become more at ease with the procedure.

In small claims court, a consumer can do a good job by going before the judge and telling the story of his or her complaint from the beginning. To do this easily, write down the history of your complaint. Arrange the events in the order they occurred, checking the dates. Pull together all the documents related to your claim, such as the repair orders and any service bulletins. If the record keeping system in Chapter Three is followed, the important papers needed to show your side of the story will be readily available.

The most valuable evidence is documentation showing that the defect on your car is covered by a secret warranty. Most importantly, you should get copies of the service bulletins relating to the defect on your make and model vehicle. Also obtain information on other complaints similar to yours from NHTSA to help demonstrate the widespread nature of the problem. See Chapter Three above.

Where possible, get written statements or affidavits from a car mechanic that state that the problem on your car is the defect covered by the secret warranty. If the mechanic is willing, have his statement notarized by a notary public. Also where possible, bring physical evidence (broken or defective parts) of the defect.

The vast majority of small claims suits are decided without witnesses. If you do bring witnesses, make arrangements with them prior to the hearing. It is best to get a witness to testify at the hearing on a voluntary basis rather than by court order. If the witness is not willing to come to the hearing, ask the witness to make a written statement or affidavit indicating his or her knowledge of the case.

In the rare case where success depends upon a witness actually appearing in court, and the witness will not come voluntarily, check with the court clerk to see if the small claims court has subpoena power (ability to order a witness to appear in court). The people to subpoena are: 1) the dealer's service manager who is the one the auto company notifies at the dealership about secret warranties; 2) the factory zone or regional representative; and 3) the mechanics at the dealership who repaired the car if they said the failure of a part was due to a manufacturing defect.

If the court can issue subpoenas, check to see if the court can issue a "subpoena duces tecum" which means the party subpoenaed must bring relevant documents which you specify. The documents you want are the policy and technical service bulletins related to the defects in your car, the complete list of all policy adjustments or secret warranties affecting your car, and the car company's current list of all policy adjustments or secret warranties. Most auto companies will immediately settle the case if the court issues such a subpoena.

Settlement

Many small claims suits based on valid secret warranty claims are settled out of court before they can come to trial. Once a manufacturer sees that a consumer means business by going to small claims court or beyond, he or she frequently agrees to meet the consumer's demands. Nancy Chasen told CAS about her success in settling:

> The metallic blue paint on my Ford Mustang started flaking off after the original warranty expired. I complained to the dealer who set up an appointment for me to see the factory representative. The rep. admitted my car had defective paint but that I would have to pay for repainting the car since the warranty had expired. I told her the Center for Auto Safety said there was a secret warranty on Fords with metallic blue paint. Confronted with my information, Ford agreed to pay half the cost but I was still

out a thousand dollars since the whole car had to be stripped and repainted.

I rejected Ford's offer and filed suit in small claims court. Ford called me and increased their offer to 75% of the cost. I told him I would see them in court before I accepted a dollar less than the complete cost of repainting the car. The morning before the trial, a lawyer representing Ford called me up and said Ford would pay the whole $2000 plus bill if I agreed to dismiss the case. I told him to put it in writing and have it at my office that afternoon. He did and we settled.

Thank you Center for Auto Safety. Tell other consumers to stick to their guns when they know there is a secret warranty and the auto company will pay up.

> N. Chasen
> Arlington, Virginia

You can even settle in the courtroom on the day of the hearing before court actually begins. Some courts have clerks, other assistants or even judges available to expedite this settlement process before trial. A few courts will make small claims parties meet in a settlement room before going into the courtroom.

If you want to settle, be prepared to bargain. Make sure you understand all the terms before you settle and get the terms of the settlement in writing. Do not settle for anything you feel is unfair. Upon settlement, file a copy signed by both parties with the court so that the settlement can be enforced by law. If the court allows, arrange to appear in court to clarify with the judge the settlement terms. Insist on reimbursement of court costs as part of the settlement.

The Hearing
If there is no settlement, you will have your day in court. Most small claims courts call the roll of cases and parties at the begin-

ning before taking each case in order. If a party is late or does not appear, the case can be decided immediately in favor of the party who is present, so be on time. Roman Malinowski of Alpena, Michigan got a default judgment of $466.88 against General Motors to repaint the roof on his Chevrolet truck when General Motors failed to show up at the court hearing.

When the clerk calls your case the judge will ask each party to tell his or her side of the story. In the course of presenting your case, give the court copies of any written evidence you have. If you have any witnesses, call them before the judge and ask them to tell what they know. The judge will not expect you to have any legal knowledge; he or she will merely ask you to state the facts as clearly and concisely as you can. The judge will ask questions to clarify anything that was not clearly presented. The other party will then be given an opportunity to present his or her side. Many small claims courts have cross examination of witnesses only, not the parties. The following suggestions will help you present your case at the hearing:

Rehearse your presentation before going to court. If you know your case well, you should be able to present the facts easily and with confidence.

Provide the court and the auto manufacturer's representative with a copy of your repair order(s) (with cancelled check(s) attached). Label each submission with corresponding exhibit letters (A, B, C, etc.) so they can be easily referenced.

Bring copies of supporting documentation of your car's defects/secret warranties, including recalls, service bulletins, studies, articles, fact sheets, and similar consumer complaints to present to the judge and the opposing party. Label each with exhibit letters as well.

Be as organized as possible. Have a summary listing of each breakdown or repair, together with the relevant date and mileage indicated in each entry. Repair information should include the garage's diagnosis, the repair work actually done, the repair order number, and the amount you paid for each repair.

When asked questions during the hearing, take a moment to think about how to respond, especially if the other party is questioning you. They may try to phrase their questions so that the only reply you can give will sound damaging. Rephrase the question to expose this tactic and respond accordingly.

The judge may give a decision at the hearing, or notify the parties of the decision by mail. If you lose, you may have the right to appeal; if you win, the defendant may be able to appeal. Check with the clerk about the appeal procedure (see Appendix F).

Arbitration

Some court systems provide for arbitration instead of or in addition to small claims courts. (See Appendix F for a list of jurisdictions where this is an option.) Both are similar, the main difference being that in arbitration one goes before an arbitrator rather than a judge. This method enabled a Buffalo, New York couple to get $780 from General Motors for the repairs and other expenses incurred when their Oldsmobile Cutlass broke down. The DiDomenico family was on a motor trip when the engine in their Cutlass failed and had to be completely rebuilt at a cost of $540. They had to cancel their vacation plans, rent a car and return home. Although the car had just over 13,000 miles on it, the manufacturer's district representative refused to make any adjustment. The DiDomenicos threatened legal action and would have settled for a smaller amount than what they actually ended up winning in small claims court. But General Motors remained unresponsive. A local legal aid office suggested suing General Motors in small claims court which used judicial arbitration.

In Mrs. DiDomenico's own words:

> This entire experience was frightening, inasmuch as we had never been involved in a lawsuit; consequently we

had no lawyer to ask for advice, and we felt completely helpless dealing with this giant corporation.

Throughout, a pattern emerged whereby my husband would first try to reach an agreeable settlement by telephone or in person, and he would be given sympathetic understanding and be temporarily pacified, first by the dealer/repairman, then by the Olds Division representative, then by the Olds Division in Lansing, Michigan, and by the local dealer from whom we had purchased the car. But in each instance a point was reached where they turned off, became unavailable, unresponsive.

After we had threatened legal action and they didn't offer to settle (we would have accepted just about any reasonable amount: $200 or $300) we seemed to have no alternative but to go ahead. It was as if they were calling our bluff, daring us to take General Motors to court.

Armed with receipts to show proper maintenance, motel accommodations when they were stranded, rental car fees, long distance phone calls and the repair bill itself, they submitted their claim to an arbitrator provided by the court. General Motors had a lawyer to present its case and even brought an expert witness to testify on its behalf. The DiDomenicos had no lawyer, but they did have good records and concrete evidence (the engine parts which had to be replaced) to give credibility to their case. They were awarded full recovery: $780 from General Motors.

Mrs. DiDomenico sent her advice to other consumers in a letter to CAS:

In retrospect I would say that it is most important to keep complete, accurate records of all work done on the car. In case of a problem, speak directly to the proper person and be persistent and don't back off.

Small claims court is the best possible place for the

average consumer to take his legal matter. Every conceivable type person was among those filling the courtroom: individuals suing individuals (some still arguing), individuals having complaints against businesses, many businesses represented by lawyers.

A clerk called the docket to first determine whether anyone had failed to show up, and when General Motors was called, there was such a gasp of reaction in the room that we couldn't hear the response. But of course they were present and we both agreed to an arbitrator. We did have a completely fair and thorough opportunity to have it all out.

Finally, small claims court is the place for the consumer to have his faith in equal justice restored. Every person should make it a point just to visit his local Small Claims Court one day and realize it is not necessary to have legal knowledge or a lawyer to have his chance to get a fair hearing.

Auto manufacturers should be held responsible for defective products. They should not be allowed to discriminate between their customers in the implementation of their secret warranties. Your persistence can ensure you get the benefit of the manufacturer's secret warranty. And small claims court could provide you with the most effective forum in which to achieve your objective.

Collecting the Judgment

While some consumers who win in small claims court do not always collect the full amount of the award, this should never be the case with a giant auto company whose assets run into the billions. Auto companies can hardly say they don't have the funds to pay judgments on secret warranties that seldom exceed a couple thousand dollars. Nonetheless, sometimes they fail to pay promptly so a little collection advice is helpful.

The court is not responsible for the actual collection of judgments but it can help enforce the judgment. At the hearing, ask the judge to order the entire amount to be paid at one time in a single payment. If notification is by mail, contact the defendant and ask for the money. If the defendant does not pay within a reasonable time (2–3 weeks), go back to the small claims court clerk. Fill out the necessary forms and the clerk will tell you how to get a sheriff or marshall to collect the money owed by the defendant. The cost of a sheriff or marshall can be added to your judgment. File with the clerk a list of all the costs accumulated in trying to collect the judgment.

If the sheriff or marshall cannot collect the money owed to you, ask the court clerk for information about what to do next. If an oral examination of the defendant is possible, request a hearing before a judge to decide what action can be taken to make the defendant pay the judgment. At the hearing, you can find out what local assets the auto company has that can be attached such as payments to a dealer or vehicles that have not yet been sold to the dealer. Just think what fun it would be to have the local news cover a marshall serving a writ of attachment on a truckload of new $60,000 Corvettes being delivered to the local Chevrolet dealer. The clerk can help you fill out the necessary forms for the writ.

Persistence does pay off, as one consumer proved when he sued the Ford Motor Company. Bob Repas of East Lansing, Michigan had a serious rusting problem with the tailgate of his Ford station wagon. The difficulty began when the car was new and continued to get worse despite frequent trips to the shop for repairs. By the time the car was only three years old, the entire tailgate was rusted and required replacement at a cost of $291.90. Mr. Repas won his case and was awarded a total of $305.30, with the extra $13.40 for court costs. However, Ford stalled for several months before paying. After additional hearings he received the original judgment plus 74 days interest on the sum.

Mr. Repas wrote in a letter to CAS:

> I am most irked about the way this company stalled on paying the judgment . . . It is determined to give anyone a hard time who doesn't accept their verdict as final and infallible.

Mr. Repas's persistence made him a winner.

Suing without a Lawyer

Even where nearby small claims courts do exist, some consumers file suit in a higher court because the jurisdictional amount (limit on the amount you can recover in a given court) is too low or service cannot be obtained in small claims court. In order to avoid legal fees, some consumers have pursued the case on their own, without hiring a lawyer. Others did so because they couldn't find a lawyer willing to take on an auto manufacturer.

One example is Toby Cagan who took Chrysler Corporation to court and won—without a lawyer—an award for her defective Dodge Aspen. She had complained over and over again about her "lemon" to Chrysler dealers and to the manufacturer, but Chrysler treated her complaints callously, responding with form letters and rude, reluctant service.

Before Cagan signed for her Aspen, she took a test drive and found many problems with the car, including difficult steering, sticky windows and doors, stalling, and dents. When she complained to the salesperson he told her that, "It's a new car and these problems have to work themselves out." Trusting the salesperson at his word, Cagan drove away in her new Dodge. When the car developed more problems within a week, she took the car back to the dealer. For the next several months, Cagan tried to get six different Chrysler dealerships to repair her car, but still without satisfaction. She sent letters and made telephone calls to Chrysler. All she received was the run-around. By this time, the consumer was quite angry. "The car had been defective since the date of its purchase. After three government recalls, numerous problems, and defects, I was afraid to drive the car," she said.

So Toby Cagan filed a lawsuit against Chrysler Corporation in Civil Court, in the city of Queens, New York. Having planned ahead, she had saved all the repair orders to document her "lemon" story, showing how she had brought the car into numerous Chrysler service departments again and again with no success. Chrysler simply could not fix her car. As her story unfolded in the courtroom, the shabby treatment Chrysler gave the consumer was exposed. She brought in a mechanic to verify the defects in the engine and drive-train. A body shop owner testified that her car had formed rust.

Cagan also brought in reports from the Center for Auto Safety, describing how CAS had written to Chrysler's Chairman about the large number of complaints on the Aspens and the identical Volares. Most of the complaints, which were similar to those Cagan had experienced, concerned carburetor, brake, drive-line, and steering problems. (Chrysler had earlier denied CAS' charges, calling the group's claims "irresponsible." But within the next six months, Chrysler had initiated four large recalls for the very same defects experienced by consumers writing to CAS and Ralph Nader. (About 80% of all Aspen and Volare owners had their cars subject to all four recalls.)

Although Chrysler brought in an expensive New York City lawyer, its only witness was a zone official who admitted, incredibly, that the car was defective, as Cagan claimed, but that given enough opportunities Chrysler could fix all the defects. After hearing Cagan's witnesses at the trial, Chrysler gave in and offered to refund the consumer's purchase price minus $500 for the 18 months she had owned the car.

William McHugh was another consumer who had success against an automaker in small claims court. He recovered over $2,700 (including costs on his claim) to repaint his Ford F-150 truck. He wrote to CAS of his small claims court success:

> April 18, 1993
> After 10 months and help from CAS I've received a favorable decision in Small Claims Court regarding Ford's paint peel on my F-150. . . .
> Thanks again for all your valuable help in this case.
>
> Sincerely,
> W. T. McHugh
> Walnut Creek, California

Cagan, McHugh, and other consumers who do not give up easily prove that you don't always need a lawyer to take a giant corporation to court and win. But you do need persistence and planning. Toby Cagan and William McHugh had plenty of both, much to the dismay of Chrysler and Ford. Their experience is an example for all that the consumer *can* win out over injustice.

BRIEF DESCRIPTION OF SOME OF THE ARBITRATION PROGRAMS AND ARBITRATION PROGRAMS BY AUTO COMPANY

AUTOCAP

In 1974, the U.S. Office of Consumer Affairs encouraged the Automotive Trade Association Managers (ATAM) and the National Automobile Dealers Association (NADA) to set up the Automotive Consumer Action Program (AUTOCAP). AUTOCAP exists in 26 states primarily in large metropolitan areas. (See p. 205 for list of participating states.) Where one exists, the local AUTOCAP may help you and the dealer settle the complaint. As a result of this first step, only 20 percent of all cases go to a panel. If the parties cannot agree, the case goes before the panel—usually without your having to appear in person. If the consumer does not attend a panel meeting, the dealer is not permitted to and the panel makes a recommendation on the basis of written information alone. Decisions by the panel are not legally binding for either the dealer or the consumer, however the program has experienced a fairly high compliance rate on the part of dealers when a recommendation is made that is not in their favor.

The average panel has nine members: six "consumer representatives" and three dealers. This method of resolving auto complaints will resolve some complaints. But the panels will not resolve the worst cases or the genuine lemon and not all manufactures endorse AUTOCAP as their dispute resolution mechanism, relying instead on a self-monitoring device such as Ford's Dispute Settlement Board.

DISPUTE SETTLEMENT BOARD

In September 1977, Ford Motor Co. began a program to help resolve its consumer service complaints: a five-member consumer complaint panel, called the Ford Consumer Appeals Board (now called the Dispute Settlement Board). The Board meets on a local level once a month, without presentation from the dealer or consumer involved. Unlike the AUTOCAP program, any decision by the Ford board will be binding on the company and the dealer. But decisions of the Board are not binding on the consumer who is free to take further action if he or she so desires. The boards are usually made up of two dealers, a state official, a vocational educator and a "consumer advocate." It is important to note that the Board will not hear complaints which are not within the terms of a new vehicle warranty and which involve personal or property damage, or sales and delivery problems. It also will not hear complaints where the consumer no longer owns the vehicle or is currently in litigation over the vehicle.

BETTER BUSINESS BUREAU

The Better Business Bureau (BBB) conducts an Auto Line arbitration program which is used by eleven auto companies: General Motors, American Motors, Nissan, Volkswagon/Audi, Porsche, Honda/Acura, Rolls Royce, Subaru, Saab, Toyota/Lexus, Hyundai, and Suzuki. Consumers who submit to BBB are given a list of arbitrators and may rank them according to preference. You also have a choice of having your case decided through written submissions, a hearing conducted over the telephone, or an oral hearing, where both you and the auto manufacturer's representative appear in person. The decision made by the arbitrator is binding on the manufacturer but not the consumer, who may reject it and pursue other remedies. This program also operates at no cost to the consumer. To be eligible for the BBB program, a consumer's vehicle must not exceed the mileage and age limits set by the manufacturer. The manufacturers' mileage and age limits vary.

CHRYSLER CUSTOMER ARBITRATION BOARD

The CCAS is also a third party body established to resolve consumer complaints free of charge. Like the Ford Board, the CCAB does not hear disputes regarding the sale of new or used cars, the design of a vehicle or its components, or a case in litigation. Although the dealer is bound by any decision, the consumer is free to pursue other means of recourse. The Board is composed of three voting members: a local consumer advocate, an independent technical representative certified by the National Institute of Automotive Service Excellence, and a representative from the general public. The Board promises that a written decision will be issued within 40 days.

ARBITRATION PROGRAMS BY AUTO COMPANY

Acura—BBB
Alfa Romeo—BBB
Audi—BBB
BMW—BBB, involved in arbitration programs run by about 10 states
Chrysler—Chrysler Customer Arbitration Board
Fiat—AUTOCAP
Ford—Dispute Settlement Board
General Motors—BBB
Honda—BBB
Hyundai—BBB

Appendix A

Infiniti—BBB
Isuzu—BBB
Jaguar—Jaguar Cars **Arbitration**
Land Rover—BBB
Lexus—BBB
Maserati—Chrysler Customer Arbitration Board
Mazda—participates in arbitration programs required by states
Mitsubishi—BBB
Nissan—BBB
Peugeot—BBB
Porsche—BBB
Rolls-Royce—BBB
Saab—BBB
Saturn—BBB
Subaru—BBB
Suzuki—BBB
Toyota—BBB
Volkswagen—BBB
Volvo—AUTOCAP, state arbitration programs

**ADDRESSES OF
ARBITRATION PROGRAMS**
Dispute Settlement Board
P.O. Box 5120
Southfield, MI 48086-5120

If a Ford consumer has questions about a case he or she has already initiated with the Dispute Settlement Board, he or she can call 1-800-428-3718.

Chrysler Customer Arbitration Board:
Box 1919
Detroit, MI 48288
1-800-992-1997

Better Business Bureau
Contact your local BBB or
Better Business Bureau (Main Office):
Council of Better Business Bureaus
4200 Wilson Blvd., Suite 800
Arlington, VA 22203
703 276-0100
1-800-955-5100

AUTOCAP
8400 Westpark Drive
McLean, VA 22102
703-821-7144

The National Automobile Dealers Association sponsors the
AUTOCAP program in 26 states, listed below. The Washington,
D.C. program serves the Washington metropolitan area:

Playa del Rey, California
San Diego, California
Denver, Colorado
Jacksonville, Florida
Miami, Florida
West Palm Beach, Florida
Atlanta, Georgia
Honolulu, Hawaii
Springfield, Illinois
Lexington, Kentucky
Augusta, Maine
Rockville, Maryland
East Lansing, Michigan
Helena, Montana
Concord, New Hampshire

Appendix A

Alburquerque, New Mexico
Albany, New York (There are two Autocaps in Albany).
Binghamton, New York
Whitestone, New York
Williamsville, New York
Rochester, New York
Raleigh, North Carolina
Fargo, North Dakota
Cleveland, Ohio
Columbus, Ohio
Tulsa, Oklahoma
Portland, Oregon
Warwick, Rhode Island
Columbia, South Carolina
Sioux Falls, South Dakota
Austin, Texas
Montpelier, Vermont
Madison, Wisconsin

STATES WHICH CERTIFY MANUFACTURERS' INFORMAL DISPUTE SETTLEMENT MECHANISMS

According to a June 1992 survey of state Attorneys General conducted by the Center for Auto Safety, the following manufacturers' informal dispute mechanisms (ISDM) are certified:

California

> *BBB/Autoline* for General Motors, Alfa Romeo, Geo, Maserati, Nissan/Infiniti, Peugeot, Range Rover, Rolls Royce, Saab, Sterling, Volkswagen and Audi;
> *Dispute Settlement Board* for Ford;
> *Chrysler Customer Arbitration Board* for Chrysler.

Connecticut

> No manufacturer's programs have been certified

Florida

> *Dispute Settlement Board* for Ford;
> *BBB/Autoline* for GM, Saab, Volkswagen/Audi, Rolls Royce, Honda/Acura, Nissan/Infiniti

Indiana

> No manufacturer's programs have been certified

Appendix B

Ohio
BBB/Autoline for Volkswagen, Audi and General Motors; Ford Consumer Appeals Board for Ford.

North Dakota
Ford Consumer Appeals Board for Ford.

Minnesota
Requires all manufacturers doing business in Minnesota to offer an arbitration program which complies with the requirements in the lemon law.

Many states do not certify IDSMs at all. The following states clearly indicated that they do not certify manufacturers' arbitration programs:

Kentucky
Maryland
North Carolina
Pennsylvania

The remainder of the states either did not respond to the survey, or responded, but did not specifically address certification of manufacturer's IDSMs.

STATE RUN ARBITRATION PROGRAMS

Connecticut*
District of Columbia
Florida*
Georgia*
Hawaii
Maine*
Massachusetts
Montana*
New Hampshire
New York
South Carolina*
Texas
Vermont
Washington

*Lemon Law requires consumers to utilize manufacturer's certified/complying mechanism before resorting to state-run arbitration.

AUTO COMPANY EXECUTIVES AND ADDRESSES

Mr. Vittorio C.Vellano
President
Alfa Romeo Distributors of North America
8259 Exchange Drive, P.O. Box 598026
Orlando, FL 32859-8026

Mr. Koichi Amemiya
President
American Honda Motor Co. Inc.
1919 Torrance Boulevard
Torrance, CA 90501-2746

Mr. Walter Hayes
Chairman and CEO
Aston Martin Lagonda of North America Inc.
1290 East Main Street
Stamford, CT 06902

Mr. Clive Warrilow
Chairman and CEO
Audi of America Inc.
3800 Hamlin Road
Auburn Hills, MI 48326

Appendix D

Mr. Victor H. Doolan
President
BMW of North America Inc.
300 Chestnut Ridge Road
Woodcliff Lake, NJ 07675

Mr. Robert Eaton
CEO
Chrysler Corporation
12000 Chrysler Drive
Highland Park, MI 48288-1919

Mr. Gian Luigi Longinotti **Buitoni**
President and COO
Ferrari North America Inc.
250 Sylvan Avenue
Englewood Cliffs, NJ 07632

Mr. Alex Trotman
Chairman and CEO
Ford Motor Company
The American Road
Dearborn, MI 48121

Mr. John F. Smith, Jr.
President and CEO
General Motors Corporation
General Motors Building
Detroit, MI 48202

Mr. Doug Mazza
Executive Vice President and COO
Hyundai Motor America
10550 Talbert Avenue
Fountain Valley, CA 92728

Mr. Kozo Sakaino
President
American Isuzu Motors Inc.
13181 Crossroads Pkwy. N., 4th Floor
City of Industry, CA 91746

Mr. Michael H. Dale
President
Jaguar Cars
555 MacArthur Boulevard
Mahwah, NJ 07430-2327

Mr. H. R. Park
President
Kia Motors America Inc.
2 Cromwell
P.O. Box 52410
Irvine, CA 92619-2410

Mr. Setiawan Djody
Chairman and CEO
Lamborghini USA Inc.
7601 Centurion Parkway
Jacksonville, FL 32256

Mr. Charles R. Hughes
President
Land Rover North America, Inc.
4390 Parliament Place
P.O. Box 1503
Lanham, MD 20706

Appendix D

Mr. James R. Blackwell
CEO
Lotus Cars U.S.A. Inc.
1655 Lakes Parkway
Lawrenceville, GA 30243

Mr. Mario Tozzi-Condivi
Chairman and CEO
Maserati Automobiles Inc.
1501 Caton Avenue
Baltimore, MD 21227

Mr. Kazuo Sonoguchi
President and CEO
Mazda Motor of America Inc.
7755 Irvine Center Drive
Irvine, CA 92630

Mr. Michael Bassermann
CEO
Mercedes-Benz of North America Inc.
P.O. Box 350
1 Mercedes Drive
Montvale, NJ 07645-0350

Mr. Tohei Takeuchi
President and CEO
Mitsubishi Motor Sales of America Inc.
6400 Katella Avenue
Cypress, CA 90630

Mr. Robert J. Thomas
President and CEO

Nissan Motor Corp. In U.S.A.
18501 S. Figueroa St.
Carson, CA 90248-0191

Mr. Serge Banzet
President
Peugeot Motors of America Inc.
1 Peugeot Plaza
Lyndhurst, NJ 07071

Mr. Frederick J. Schwab
President and CEO
Porsche Cars North America Inc.
100 West Liberty Street
Reno, NV 89501

Mr. Robert R. Wharen
Managing Director
Rolls-Royce Motor Cars Inc.
120 Chubb Avenue
P.O. Box 476
Lyndhurst, NJ 07071

Mr. James Crumlish
CEO
Saab Cars USA Inc.
4405-A Saab Drive
P.O. Box 9000
Norcross, GA 30091

Mr. Takeshi Higurashi
Chairman and CEO
Subaru of America Inc.

Appendix D

Subaru Plaza
P.O. Box 6000
Cherry Hill, NJ 08034-6000

Mr. Yoshinosi Fujii
President
American Suzuki Motors Corporation
3251 E. Imperial Hwy.
Brea, CA 92621-6722

Mr. Shinji Sakai
President and CEO
Toyota Motors Sales U.S.A. Inc.
19001 S. Western Avenue
Torrance, CA 90509

Mr. Clive Warrilow
President
Volkswagen of America Inc.
3800 Hamlin Road
Auburn Hills, MI 48326

Mr. Mats-Ola Palm
Chairman and CEO
Volvo Cars of North America Inc.
P.O. Box 913
1 Volvo Drive
Rockleigh, NJ 07647

FEDERAL GOVERNMENT ADDRESSES

The White House
1600 Pennsylvania Avenue, NW
Washington, DC 20500
(202) 456-1414
> White House Office of Consumer Affairs (202) 634-4310

Agencies:

Department of Energy
1000 Independence Avenue, SW
Washington, DC 20585
(202) 586-5000

Department of Transportation
National Highway Traffic Safety Administration
400 Seventh Street, SW
Washington, DC 20590
TOLL-FREE HOTLINE (800) 424-9393/from anywhere outside
> Washington, DC
> call 366-0123 from within the DC Metropolitan area
> TTY(800) 424-9153/from anywhere outside Washington, DC
> call 366-7800 from within the DC Metropolitan area
> Administrator (202) 366-1836
> Director, Office of Defects Investigation (202) 366-2850

Appendix E

Environmental Protection Agency
401 M Street, SW
Washington, DC 20460
(202) 260-2090
 Office of Mobile Sources (202) 260-7645

Federal Trade Commission
Bureau of Consumer Protection
6th and Pennsylvania Avenue, NW
Washington, DC 20580
(202) 326-2000

Congressional Committees:

Committee on Commerce, Science, and Transportation
U.S. Senate
Washington, DC 20510
(202) 224-5115
 Consumer Subcommittee (202) 224-0415

Committee on Energy and Commerce
U.S. House of Representatives
Washington, DC 20515
(202) 225-2927
 Subcommittees on: Commerce, Consumer Protection, and Competitiveness (202) 226-3160
 Telecommunications and Finance (202) 226-2424

Individual Members of Congress:

Senator: The Honorable (full name)
             U.S. Senate
             Washington, DC 20510

Representative: The Honorable (full name)
                U.S. House of Representatives
                Washington, DC 20515

Call (202) 224-3121 (Capitol switchboard) and ask for your senator or representative.

SMALL CLAIMS COURT DIRECTORY

State	Type of Court	Claim Limit	Informal Procedure?	Lawyers Allowed?	Appeal	Dispute Resolution?
Alabama	Small Claims Docket in District Court	$1,500	Yes	Yes	Either party within 14 days to Circuit Court for new trial.	No
Alaska	Small Claims	$5,000	Yes	Yes	Yes	No
Arizona	Justice Court Small Claims Division	$1,500 Small Claims Division: $5,000 regular Justice Court	No	Yes if both parties agree in writing	No: Small Claims Division Yes: Justice Court	Commission on the Courts: Task Force on Dispute Resoluion
Arkansas	Municipal Court Small Claims Division	$3,000	Yes	No	Either party within 30 days to Circuit Court for new trial	No
California	Small Claims Division in Municipal or Justice Court	$5,000	Yes	No	Defendant (or plaintiff who lost on a counter-claim) within 30 days to Superior Court for new trial	Varies from county to county
Colorado	County Court Small Claims Division	$3,500	Yes	No, unless the case is in County Court.	Either party within 15 days to District Court on law not facts	No

Appendix F

State	Type of Court	Claim Limit	Informal Procedure?	Lawyers Allowed?	Appeal	Dispute Resolution?
Connecticut	Small Claims in Superior Court	$2,000	Yes	Yes	No	No
Delaware	Justice of the Peace	$5,000	Yes	Yes	Either party within 15 days to Superior Court for new trial if over $5	No
District of Columbia	Small Claims and conciliation Branch within Civil Division of Superior Court	$2,000	Yes	Yes and corpora-tions are required to be rep-resented by an attorney	Either party within 10 days to trial court if judgment by hearing commissioner; either party within 30 days to Court of Appeals if judgment by judge	Yes, mandatory Mediation.
Florida	Small Claims Court	$2500	Yes	Yes	Motion for new trial within 10 days; Either party appeal within 30 days to Circuit Court on law not facts	Usually Yes
Georgia	Magistrate Court	$5,000	Yes	Yes	To Superior Court for new trial	Local Option
Hawaii	Small Claims Division in District Court	$3,500	Yes	Yes	No	Program on Alternative Dispute Resolution
Idaho	Small Claims Department of Magistrate's Division in District Court	$2,000	Yes	Only for enforce-ment of a judgment	Either party within 30 days to Attorney Magistrate for new trial	No
Illinois	Small Claims Court	$2,500 small claims; $1500 Cook County "pro se"	Yes	Yes except Cook County pro se branch	Either party within 30 days to Appellate Court on law not facts	No

State	Type of Court	Claim Limit	Informal Procedure?	Lawyers Allowed?	Appeal	Dispute Resolution?
Indiana	Small Claims Court; Small Claims Docket in Circuit Court, Superior Court, and County Court	$6,000 Plus interest and attorneys fees in Marion County; $10,000 in Lake County with an attorney and $3,000 without an attorney; elsewhere, $3,000.	Yes	Yes	Yes	No
Iowa	Small Claims Docket in District Court	$3,000 and after July 1, 1995, $4,000	Yes	Yes	Either party within 20 days to District Court	Advisory Committee on Dispute Resolution
Kansas	Small Claims in District Court	$1,000	Yes	Not before judgment	Either party within 10 days to District Court for new trial	No
Kentucky	Small Claims Division in District Court	$1,500	Yes	Yes	Either party within 10 days to Circuit Court on law not facts	No (Court on law not facts)
Louisiana	Urban: City Court Small Claims Division. Rural: Justice of the Peace	$2,000 Small Claims; $1,500 Justice of the Peace	Yes	Yes	No for Small Claims; yes if transferred to regular docket	No
Maine	Small Claims in District Court	$3,000	Yes	Yes	Either party within 30 days to Superior Court. If plaintiff appeals, on law only. If defendant appeals, defendant has option of a jury trial.	Yes
Maryland	Small Claims Action in District Court	$2,500	Yes	Yes	Either party within 30 days to Circuit Court for new trial	yes

Appendix F

State	Type of Court	Claim Limit	Informal Procedure?	Lawyers Allowed?	Appeal	Dispute Resolution?
Massachusetts	Small Claims Court (Boston —Municipal Court; Elsewhere—District Court)	$2,000, except for property damages caused by a motor vehicle or when double or triple damages are permitted by law	Yes	Yes	Defendent always has right to appeal within 10 days to Superior Court for new trial; $100 bond or cash or check required.	Yes
Michigan	Small Claims Division in District Court	$1,750	Yes	No	Depends	No
Minnesota	Conciliation Court in District Court	$7,500	Yes	Need Court approval	Within 20 days to District Court	Yes, varies from county to county
Mississippi	Justice Court	$1,000	Yes	Yes	Either party within 10 days to circuit court for new trial	No
Missouri	Small Claims Court in Circuit Court	$1,500	Yes	Yes	Either party within 10 days for new trial	No
Montana	Small Claims Court in Justice Court	$3,000	Yes	Only if all parties present have attorneys	Either party within 30 days if District Court for new trial or 10 days if Justice Court on law not facts	No
Nebraska	Small Claims Court in County or Municipal Court	$1,800	Yes	No	Either party within 30 days to District Court	No
Nevada	Small Claims in Justice Court	$3,500	No	Yes	Either party within 20 days to District Court on law not facts	No
New Hampshire	Small Claims Actions in District or Municipal Court	$2,500	Yes	Yes	Either party within 30 days to Supreme Court on law not facts	Yes

State	Type of Court	Claim Limit	Informal Procedure?	Lawyers Allowed?	Appeal	Dispute Resolution?
New Jersey	Small Claims Section which is Special Civil Part of Law Division of Superior Court	$7,500	Yes	Yes	Either party within 45 days to Appellate Division of Superior Court on law not facts	Center for Public Dispute Resolution
New Mexico	Urban: Metropolitan Court; Rural: Magistrate's Court	$5,000 Magistrate's Court; $5,000 Metropolitan Court	Yes	Yes	Either party within 15 days to District Court	Yes
New York	Small Claims in Civil Court, District Court & Justice Court	$2,000	Yes	Yes	Defendant within 30 days to County Court or Appellate Division on law not facts; Plaintiff only on the ground that "substantial justice" was not done	Yes
North Carolina	Small Claims Actions in **District** Court	$3,000	Yes	Yes	Either party within 10 days to District Court for new trial	No
North Dakota	**Small Claims** Court	$3,000	**Yes**	**Yes**	No	No
Ohio	Small Claims in Municipal and County Courts	$2,000 for claims; $2,000 for counter-claims; $3,000 in County Court	Yes	Yes	Within 30 days to Court of Appeals	Yes
Oklahoma	Small Claims in District Court	$2,500	Yes	Yes	Either party within 30 days to Supreme Court on law not facts	Dispute Resolution Advisory Council
Oregon	Small Claims Department in District or Justice Courts	$2,500	Yes	Need judge's consent	District Court: No Justice Court: Defendant (or plaintiff on counterclaim) 10 days to Circuit Court for new trial	Dispute Resolution Advisory Council

Appendix F

State	Type of Court	Claim Limit	Informal Procedure?	Lawyers Allowed?	Appeal	Dispute Resolution?
Pennsylvania	Philadelphia: Municipal Court; Elsewhere: District or Justice Court	$5,000 Municipal Court; District or Justice Court	Yes in Municipal Court; No in District or Justice Court	Yes	Either party within 30 days to Court of Common Pleas for new trial	Council of Mediators
Rhode Island	Small Claims in District Court	$1,500	Yes	Yes	Defendant (or Plaintiff who lost on a counterclaim) within 2 days, excluding weekends, to Superior Court for new trial	No
South Carolina	Magistrate's Court (no small claims procedure)	$2,500	No	Yes	Within 30 days to County or Circuit Court on law not facts	No
South Dakota	Small Claims Procedure in Circuit or Magistrate's Court	$4,000	Yes	Yes	No	No
Tennessee	Court of General Sessions (no small claims procedure)	$10,000.	Yes	Yes	Either party to Circuit Court for new trial	No
Texas	Small Claims Court in Justice Court	$5,000	Yes	Yes	Either party within 10 days to County Court for new trial	Yes
Utah	Small Claims in Circuit or Justice Court	$5,000	Yes	Yes	Either party within 10 days to District Court for new trial	Yes
Vermont	Small Claims Procedure in District Court	$2,000	Yes	Yes	Either party within 30 days to Superior Court on law not facts	Yes
Virginia	Small Claims in Civil Court	$10,000	Yes	Yes	Either party within 10 days to Circuit Court for new trial	Yes
Washington	Small Claims in District Court	$2,500	Yes	No	Not by a party whose claim was under $1,000. In other cases, either party within 14 days to Superior Court for new trial.	Yes

State	Type of Court	Claim Limit	Informal Procedure?	Lawyers Allowed?	Appeal	Dispute Resolution?
West Virginia	Magistrate's Court	$5,000	Yes	Yes	Either party within 20 days to Circuit Court for new trial	No
Wisconsin	Small Claims in Circuit Court	$4,000	Yes	Yes	Depends, but usually either party within 45 days to Court of Appeals on law not facts	Yes
Wyoming	County Court or Justice of the Peace Court Code	$2,000: $7,000 in City Court	Yes	Yes	Either party within 10 days to District Court on law not facts	No

SAMPLE SMALL CLAIMS
COURT COMPLAINT

Superior Court of the District of Columbia

Small Claims Form 11:

CIVIL DIVISION

General

SMALL CLAIMS AND CONCILIATION BRANCH
500 Indiana Ave., N.W.   Room JM-260
WASHINGTON, D.C. 20001   TELEPHONE 879-1120

(YOUR FULL NAME)
_____
Plaintiff

(YOUR PRESENT ADDRESS)
_____

vs.

(NAME OF THE PERSON, COMPANY OR
(1) CORPORATION YOU ARE SUING)

(FULL NAME OF 2ND DEFENDANT--IF
(2) YOU HAVE MORE THAN ONE DEFENDANT)

(FULL NAME OF 3RD DEFENDANT--IF
(3) YOU HAVE THREE DEFENDANTS)
Defendant

_____   _____
Address   Zip Code

Phone No. (YOUR HOME OR BUSINESS)No. SC (LEAVE BLANK)

STATEMENT OF CLAIM
(BRIEFLY STATE THE FACTS OF YOUR CASE AND INCLUDE DATES AND PLACES OF OCCURRENCE.
THEN DEPENDING ON THESE FACTS, YOU SHOULD MAKE AT LEAST SOME OF THE FOLLOWING
ALLEGATIONS:
    THE MANUFACTURER IS VIOLATING (1) THE STATE LAW REQUIRING DISCLOSURE OF SECRET
    WARRANTIES; (2) THE STATE UNFAIR AND DECEPTIVE TRADE PRACTICES ACT; (3) THE
    MAGNUSON-MOSS WARRANTY ACT; AND (4) THE IMPLIED WARRANTY OF MERCHANTIBILITY.
THEN LIST THE DAMAGES YOU ARE SEEKING. THEY SHOULD AT A MINIMUM INCLUDE THE COSTS
OF REPAIR AND ALTERNATE TRANSPORTATION, COURT COSTS, ATTORNEYS' FEES, AND WITNESS'
FEES.)
DISTRICT OF COLUMBIA, ss: (PRINT YOUR NAME HERE) _____ being first duly sworn on oath says
the foregoing is a just and true statement of the amount owing by the defendant to plaintiff, exclusive of
all set-offs and just grounds of defense.

(THIS SPACE IS FOR ATTORNEYS ONLY)
_____
Attorney for Plaintiff

_____   _____
Address   Zip Code

Phone No. _____

Subscribed and sworn to before me this _____ day of _____, 19____

_____
Plaintiff (or agent)

Bar No. _____

_____
Deputy Clerk (or notary public)

NOTICE
(Check address to be used for mailing)

To:
(1) (PERSON, COMPANY OR CORP. YOU ARE SUING) (2) (NAME OF 2ND DEFENDANT
Defendant   Defendant
(DEFT'S ADDRESS WHERE CLAIM IS TO BE SERVED) (DEFT'S ADDRESS WHERE CLAIM IS TO BE SERVED)

_____   _____   _____
Home Address   Zip Code   Home Address
            (CHECK HOME OR BUSINESS ADDRESS)

_____   _____   _____
Business Address   Zip Code   Business Address

You are hereby notified that (YOUR FULL NAME)

_____ has made a claim and is requesting judgment
                                                  (THE AMOUNT IN FIGURES)
against you in the sum of (THE AMOUNT YOU ARE SUING FOR--WRITTEN OUT)Dollars ($_____),

as shown by the foregoing statement. The court will hold a hearing upon this claim on _____
(LEAVE THIS SPACE BLANK)

at 9:00 a.m. in the Small Claims and Conciliation Branch located at 500 Indiana Ave., N.W., John Marshall
level, Courtroom JM-12.

SEE REVERSE SIDE FOR COMPLETE INSTRUCTIONS

BRING THIS NOTICE WITH YOU AT ALL TIMES

Form CV(6)-471/Nov. 89 0-1616-1 wd-310

Deputy Clerk
Small Claims and Conciliation Branch

SMALL CLAIMS COURTS GUIDES

Collecting the Money
Counsel for Courts Excellence
1024 Vermont Avenue, N.W.
Suite 510
Washington, DC 20005

Everybody's Guide to Small Claims
by Ralph Warner (1991) Fifth Edition
Nolo Press
950 Parker St.
Berkeley, CA 94710

Guide to Small Claims
Montgomery County Office of Consumer Affairs
100 Maryland Ave.
Rockville, MD 20850

Inexpensive Justice: Self-representation in the Small Claims Court
by Robert L. Spurrier, Jr. (1983)
Associated Faculty Press, Inc.
New York, NY

Appendix H

Small Claims Court
HALT
Memberships Department
1319 F St. N.W.
Suite 300
Washington, DC 20004

STATE OF WISCONSIN

1991 Senate Bill 450

Date of enactment: April 30, 1992
Date of publication*: May 13, 1992

1991 Wisconsin Act 298

AN ACT *to amend* 218.01 (9) (a) 1; and *to create* 218.01 (3) (a) 40 and 218.017 of the statutes, *relating to* motor vehicle warranty adjustment programs.

The people of the state of Wisconsin, represented in senate and assembly, do enact as follows:

SECTION 1e. 218.01 (3) (a) 40 of the statutes is created to read:

218.01 (3) (a) 40. Having violated s. 218.017.

SECTION 1m. 218.01 (9) (a) 1 of the statutes is amended to read:

218.01 (9) (a) 1. A violation by any other licensee of sub. (3) (a) 4, 11, 15, 16, 17, 22, 23, 24, 26, 26m, 32, 35, 36, 37, 38 or, 39 or 40.

SECTION 1s. 218.017 of the statutes is created to read:

218.017 Motor vehicle adjustment programs. (1) DEFINITIONS. In this section:

(a) "Adjustment program" means an extended policy program under which a manufacturer undertakes to pay for all or any part of the cost of repairing, or to reimburse purchasers for all or any part of the cost of repairing, any condition that may substantially affect motor vehicle durability, reliability or performance. "Adjustment program" does not include service provided under a written warranty provided to a consumer, service provided under a safety or emission-related recall program or individual adjustments made by a manufacturer on a case-by-case basis.

(b) "Consumer" has the meaning given in s. 218.015 (1) (b).

(c) "Manufacturer" has the meaning given in s. 218.015 (1) (c).

(d) "Motor vehicle" has the meaning given in s. 218.015 (1) (d).

(e) "Motor vehicle dealer" means a motor vehicle dealer, as defined in s. 218.01 (1) (n), that sells new motor vehicles.

(2) DISCLOSURE REQUIREMENTS. (a) A manufacturer shall do all of the following:

1. Establish a procedure to inform a consumer of any adjustment program applicable to the consumer's motor vehicle and, upon request, furnish the consumer with any document issued by the manufacturer relating to any adjustment program.

2. Notify, by 1st class mail, a consumer who is eligible under an adjustment program of the condition in the motor vehicle that is covered by the adjustment program and the principal terms and conditions of the adjustment program within 90 days after the date on which the adjustment program is adopted.

3. Notify its motor vehicle dealers, in writing, of all the terms and conditions of an adjustment program within 30 days after the date on which the program is adopted.

4. If a consumer is a purchaser or lessor of a new motor vehicle, notify the consumer, in writing, of the consumer's rights and remedies under this section. The notice shall include a statement in substantially the following language: "Sometimes .... (manufacturer's name) offers a special adjustment program to pay all or part of the cost of certain repairs beyond the terms of the warranty. Check with your motor vehicle dealer to determine whether any adjustment program is applicable to your motor vehicle."

(b) If a motor vehicle dealer has been informed of an adjustment program under par. (a) 3, the motor vehicle dealer shall disclose to a consumer seeking repairs for a condition covered by the adjustment program the terms and conditions of the adjustment program.

(3) ADJUSTMENT PROGRAM REIMBURSEMENT. (a) A manufacturer who establishes an adjustment program shall implement procedures to assure reimbursement of each consumer eligible under an adjustment program who incurs expenses for repair of a condition subject to the program before acquiring knowledge of

* Section 991.11, WISCONSIN STATUTES 1989-90: Effective date of acts. "Every act and every portion of an act enacted by the legislature over the governor's partial veto which does not expressly prescribe the time when it takes effect shall take effect on the day after its date of publication as designated" by the secretary of state [the date of publication may not be more than 10 working days after the date of enactment].

the program. Reimbursement shall be consistent with the terms and conditions of the particular adjustment program.

(b) A consumer shall make a claim for reimbursement under par. (a) in writing to the manufacturer within 2 years after the date of the consumer's payment for repair of the condition. The manufacturer shall notify the consumer within 21 business days, as defined in s. 421.301 (6), after receiving a claim for reimbursement if the claim will be allowed or denied. If the claim is denied, the specific reasons for the denial shall be stated in writing.

(4) REMEDIES. In addition to pursuing any other remedy, a consumer may bring an action to recover damages caused by a violation of this section. A court shall award a consumer who prevails in such an action twice the amount of any pecuniary loss, together with costs, disbursements and reasonable attorney fees, notwithstanding s. 814.04 (1), and any equitable relief the court determines appropriate.

SECTION 2. **Effective date.** This act takes effect on the first day of the 4th month beginning after publication.

Introduction

Wisconsin Act 298—effective September 1, 1992—creates s. 218.017 of the statutes and requires motor vehicle manufacturers to notify their dealers and all eligible consumers anytime the manufacturer creates a motor vehicle warranty adjustment program.

The purpose of the law is to create equity between consumers by preventing manufacturers from offering "secret warranties" that pay for out-of-warranty vehicle repairs for some but not all consumers affected by the same vehicle defect.

"Adjustment Program" Defined

"'Adjustment Program' means an extended policy program under which a manufacturer undertakes to pay for all or part of the cost of repairing any condition that may substantially affect motor vehicle durability, reliability or performance. Adjustment program does not include service provided under a.written warranty provided to a consumer, service provided under a safety or emission-related recall program or individual adjustments made by a manufacturer on a case-by-case basis." (S. 218.017 (1) (a), Wisconsin Statutes.)

"Consumer" Defined

Under Act 298 a "consumer" is any of the following:

- The purchaser of a new motor vehicle for purposes other than resale

- A lessee of a motor vehicle under a written lease

- Anyone to whom the vehicle is transferred (for purposes other than resale) during the term of the express warranty

- Anyone who may enforce the warranty

Eligible consumers include those who no longer own the covered vehicles, as long as they owned the vehicles (for purposes other than resale) or leased the vehicles during the express warranty period.

Enforcement

Wisconsin DOT can deny, suspend or revoke the business license of a manufacturer, distributor or dealer who violates the law. Also, consumers who win in court are entitled to recover double damages caused by a violation of the law, plus costs, and attorneys' fees.

Adjustment Programs Are Optional

Manufacturers don't have to pay for repairs no longer covered under an express warranty. However, if a manufacturer pays to repair the same condition affecting reliability, durability or performance of some consumers' vehicles, the manufacturer must extend similar coverage to *all* affected consumers.

Manufacturers still decide the terms and conditions of any adjustment programs—which vehicle makes, model years, and vehicle identification numbers they will cover, and how much they will pay for repairs. Manufacturers must disclose clearly all terms and conditions of a program to dealers and consumers at the outset. Once the manufacturer establishes the terms of an adjustment program, it cannot discriminate between consumers whose vehicles are eligible under those terms.

Case-by-Case Adjustments Versus "Secret Warranty"

Because the law doesn't say how many case-by-case "individual adjustments" for the same problem or condition make up a "secret warranty" or what conditions "substantially affect" vehicle durability, reliability or performance, the courts will ultimately decide those issues. To avoid being held liable for double damages under the new law, manufacturers should use good judgment in deciding when case-by-case adjustments are developing into a "secret warranty".

The following situations probably indicate a "secret warranty" may develop or already exists, and the manufacturer should notify dealers and all eligible consumers of the terms of an adjustment program:

- Many consumers complain about the same condition affecting durability, reliability or performance of vehicles no longer under an express warranty.

- A manufacturer communicates *in writing or verbally* to its regional staff or dealers that the manufacturer in selected cases will pay for repair of a certain condition affecting durability, reliability or performance of vehicles no longer under an express warranty.

- The manufacturer or its regional staff establishes a pattern of making case-by-case adjustments for the same condition affecting vehicle durability, reliability or performance.

A manufacturer may do any of the following without creating a "secret warranty":

- Pay for repairs covered by an express warranty.

- Pay for repairs under an emission or safety-related recall program.

- Pay for repair of out-of-warranty conditions that *do not* affect vehicle reliability, durability or performance.

- Pay for repair of out-of-warranty conditions that *do* affect vehicle reliability, durability or performance in *isolated cases* as long as no *pattern* of adjustments for the same condition develops.

Manufacturer Responsibilities

Manufacturers will need to do the following in order to comply with Act 298:

- Establish a procedure for notifying consumers of any adjustment program applicable to the consumer's vehicle.

- Upon request, furnish consumers with any document issued by the manufacturer relating to *any* adjustment program.

- Within *30 days* of adopting an adjustment program, notify all of the manufacturer's motor vehicle dealers of the program terms.

- Within *30 days* of adopting an adjustment program, notify the Wisconsin Department of Transportation of the program terms.

- Within *90 days* of adopting an adjustment program, notify eligible consumers of the program terms by first class mail.

- Notify all purchasers or lessors of new motor vehicles in writing (in language prescribed by statute) of consumers' rights and remedies under this law.

- Implement procedures to assure reimbursement of each eligible consumer who incurs expenses for repair of a condition subject to the program before acquiring knowledge of the program (either because the consumer wasn't notified or the program did not yet exist). Reimbursement shall be consistent with the terms and conditions of the program.

- Establish a procedure for handling consumers' written claims for reimbursement and notifying a consumer within 21 days whether a claim will be allowed or denied and why.

Dealer Responsibilities

Any dealer who has been informed of an adjustment program must disclose to a consumer seeking repairs for a condition covered by the adjustment program the terms and conditions of the adjustment program.

Consumer Responsibilities

Any consumer seeking reimbursement for repair of a condition subject to the program prior to acquiring knowledge of the program must make a written claim for reimbursement to the manufacturer within 2 years after the date of payment for repair of the condition.

For More Information or Help

For information about this law contact the Wisconsin Department of Transportation (phone number and address below).

For information about existing adjustment programs that might apply to your vehicle, contact your dealer, your vehicle's manufacturer, or the Wisconsin Department of Transportation.

To file a complaint about a possible violation of this law, contact the Wisconsin Department of Transportation. The department will mediate disputes about manufacturer's adjustment programs or "secret warranties".

> Wisconsin Dept of Transportation
> Dealer Section, Room 806
> 4802 Sheboygan Ave, PO Box 7909
> Madison, WI 53707-7909
> (608) 266-0765

Prepared by
Cathy L. Skaar
Policy Analyst
Dealer Section
Wisconsin Dept of Transportation

August, 1992

MODEL STATE SECRET WARRANTY LAW

1. **Definitions:** As used in this section, the following words shall have the following meaning.

    (a) "Consumer" means the purchaser, other than for purposes of resale, of a motor vehicle, a lessee of a motor vehicle, any person to whom the motor vehicle is transferred, and any person entitled by the terms of the warranty or by law to enforce the obligations of the warranty.

    (b) "Manufacturer" means any person, firm, or corporation, whether resident or nonresident, that imports, manufactures, assembles or distributes motor vehicles for sale or distribution in this state.

    (c) "Dealer" means any person, firm, or corporation selling or agreeing to sell in this state one or more new motor vehicles under a retail agreement with a manufacturer, manufacturer branch, distributor, distributor branch, or agent of any of them.

    (d) "Adjustment program" means any program or policy under which a manufacturer offers to pay all or any part of the cost of repairing or to reimburse owners or dealers for all or any part of the cost of repairing a defect or condition that is beyond the terms or period of coverage of the manufacturer's express written warranty given to a consumer at the time of sale or lease of the vehicle. This definition does not include service provided under safety and emission-related recall campaigns. "Adjustment program" does not include ad hoc adjustments made by a manufacturer on a case-by-case basis.

(e) "Motor vehicle" means a motor vehicle, including motorcycles, motor homes, and off-road vehicles, which are sold in this state.

(f) "Lessee" means any person who leases a motor vehicle pursuant to a written lease that provides that the lessee is responsible for repairs to the motor vehicle.

(g) "Service bulletin" means any document issued by a manufacturer pertaining to any adjustment program or any defect or condition that may affect vehicle durability, reliability, performance, or safety.

2. Required Procedures

(a) A manufacturer shall implement a procedure in this state whereby a consumer (1) shall be informed of any adjustment program applicable to his or her motor vehicle, and (2) upon request, shall be entitled to receive a copy of any service bulletins and/or index of service bulletins.

(b) A manufacturer shall, within 60 days of the adoption of an adjustment program after this law is enacted, subject to priority for safety or emission-related recalls, notify by first-class mail all owners and lessees of motor vehicles eligible under the program of the condition giving rise to and the principal terms and conditions of the program.

(c) A manufacturer shall establish and maintain a toll-free telephone system. Such system shall provide that after obtaining the consumer's name and address and such vehicle information as is deemed necessary by the manufacturer, the manufacturer's telephone representative shall: (i) inform the consumer of the existence of any adjustment program applicable to the consumer's motor vehicle; and (ii) advise the consumer that he or she may obtain, by mail, a copy of any service bulletins after paying the specified fee, if any, or that an index thereof will be provided free. The telephone representative shall furnish the consumer with the manufacturer's address to which requests for such service bulletins or index thereof may be made.

(d) A manufacturer shall, upon written request or upon oral request received pursuant to the toll-free telephone procedure set forth in subsection 2(c), mail a copy of such service bulletins or index thereof to the consumer within 21 days from the date of receipt of a consumer's request sent to the address designated by the manufacturer for such purpose together with payment of the specified charges, if any.

(e) A manufacturer may at its option impose a charge not to exceed the reasonable cost of furnishing such service bulletins or index thereof provided that such charge is disclosed to the consumer prior to furnishing it.

(f) Within 30 days of the adoption of any new adjustment program, a manufacturer shall notify its dealers as well as the state agency responsible for administering this law, in writing, of all the program's terms and conditions.

(g) A manufacturer shall notify its dealers in writing of the toll-free telephone number required to be established pursuant to subdivision 2(c).

3. **Required Disclosures**

(a) A dealer shall conspicuously post adjustment policy programs.

(b) A dealer shall notify prospective purchasers of a vehicle, prior to entering into a contract for the sale of that motor vehicle, that upon request the dealer will provide them with information about any adjustment program applicable to that vehicle.

(c) Each manufacturer, importer, or distributor, either directly or through its authorized agent, shall give the following written notice to the original purchaser of a new motor vehicle:

"Sometimes (insert manufacturer's name) offers a special adjustment program to pay all or part of the cost of certain repairs beyond the terms of the warranty. Check with your dealer or call (insert the manufacturer's toll-free telephone number) to determine whether any adjustment program is applicable to your motor vehicle.

(d) A dealer shall disclose to a consumer seeking repairs for a particular condition at its repair shop, the principal terms and conditions of any manufacturer's adjustment program covering such condition provided the dealer has received a service bulletin concerning such adjustment program or otherwise has knowledge of it.

4. **Reimbursement**

(a) A manufacturer that establishes an adjustment program shall implement procedures to assure reimbursement of each consumer eligible under an adjustment program who incurs expenses for repair of a condition subject to the program prior to acquiring knowledge of the program. The reimbursement shall be consistent with the terms and conditions of the particular program.

(b) Any claim for reimbursement under subdivision 4(a)

shall be made in writing to the manufacturer within three years of the date of the consumer's payment for repair of the condition. The manufacturer shall notify the consumer in writing within 21 business days of receiving the claim for reimbursement whether the claim will be allowed or denied. If the claim is denied, the specific reasons for the denial shall be listed in the written notification.

5. **Enforcement By Attorney General**

(a) A violation of this chapter is an unfair and deceptive trade practice under (insert section number of state code that makes unfair and deceptive trade practices illegal).

(b) Any consumer damaged by the failure of a manufacturer, importer, distributor, or dealer to comply with this chapter may bring an action to recover damages. Judgment may be entered in an amount not to exceed three times the actual damages. In addition, attorney's fees and costs shall be awarded to any prevailing consumer based on actual time expended.

(c) Whenever there is a violation of this chapter, the attorney general of this state may apply to a court having jurisdiction to issue an injunction to enjoin and restrain the continuance of the violation. The court may issue the injunction if the defendant has been given notice of at least five days and if it appears the defendant has violated this chapter. No proof that any person has been injured by the defendant's conduct is required to issue an injunction. Whenever the court determines that a violation of this chapter has occurred, it may impose a civil penalty of not more than one thousand dollars ($1,000) for each violation. If a manufacturer adopts an adjustment policy and does not give consumers the notification required by this law, the manufacturer's conduct shall constitute one violation of this law. In connection with any such proposed application, the attorney general is authorized to take proof and make a determination of the relevant facts and to issue subpoenas in accordance with the civil practice law and rules.

(d) (Insert the name of the state agency responsible for enforcing the law) is authorized to promulgate reasonable regulations in order to implement the provisions of this law. These regulations shall be adopted, amended, or repealed in accordance with state law.

(e) Nothing in this chapter shall be construed to exclude, modify, or otherwise limit any other remedy provided by law to a consumer or lessee.

Index

Index

Index

Index

Index

Index

Index

Index

Index

CENTER FOR AUTO SAFETY MEMBERSHIP

The Center for Auto Safety (CAS) is the only consumer group working full time to disclose secret warranties by auto makers and to improve auto safety and quality. For car owners wondering whether their vehicle is covered by a secret warranty, CAS is the best source of information.

The Center for Auto Safety depends on your support in our fight for consumers against the giant car companies. Annual membership in CAS is $15, less than the price of an oil change, and is fully tax-deductible. As a CAS member you will receive our *Lemon Times* newsletter telling you about the latest secret warranties, other auto defects and consumer success stories.

CENTER FOR AUTO SAFETY   MEMBERSHIP FORM

Yes! I strongly support the work of the Center for Auto Safety to disclose secret warranties and make cars safer. Be sure to keep me informed of the CAS' actions and any new secret warranties through your quarterly newsletter, *The Lemon Times.*

___ Enclosed is my annual membership contribution of $15.

___ I want to make an additional contribution.
Enclosed is ___ $25   ___ $50   ___ $100   ___ other

Your contribution is tax-deductible.

Name: _____

Address: _____

_____

2001 S St., N.W., Suite 410, Washington, D.C. 20009